Keeping Watch for Kingfishers

God Stories

— JENNY WILSON —

Sacristy Press

Sacristy Press
PO Box 612, Durham, DH1 9HT

www.sacristy.co.uk

First published in 2020 by Sacristy Press, Durham

Copyright © Jenny Wilson 2020.
The moral rights of the author have been asserted.

All rights reserved, no part of this publication may be reproduced or transmitted in any form or by any means, electronic, mechanical photocopying, documentary, film or in any other format without prior written permission of the publisher.

Scripture quotations, unless otherwise stated, are from the New Revised Standard Version Bible: Anglicized Edition, copyright © 1989, 1995 National Council of the Churches of Christ in the United States of America. Used by permission. All rights reserved worldwide.

Every reasonable effort has been made to trace the copyright holders of material reproduced in this book, but if any have been inadvertently overlooked the publisher would be glad to hear from them.

Sacristy Limited, registered in England & Wales, number 7565667

British Library Cataloguing-in-Publication Data
A catalogue record for the book is available from the British Library

ISBN 978-1-78959-073-9

Foreword

Over the past several years, my colleagues and I at Westminster Abbey have been fortunate to get to know the Reverend Canon Jenny Wilson. The Abbey, since the time of Queen Elizabeth I more correctly named as the Collegiate Church of Saint Peter in Westminster, is a house of prayer and a house of kings, a place where God has been worshipped and adored for over a thousand years. It is a destination and a refuge for pilgrims and a church that places faith at the heart of the nation it serves. How appropriate, then, to offer a few words of introduction on behalf of a priest and precentor serving another great church dedicated to Saint Peter; in a place at once far removed from Westminster Abbey, and yet as one with it: one in apostolic patronage and one in commitment to sustaining God's people through prayer, scripture and the sacraments of the Church.

This universal call to worship the Lord God with all our heart, soul, mind and strength, and so to bring about on earth Christ's heavenly kingdom, stands at the heart of this new and much-welcomed compilation of sermons *Keeping Watch for Kingfishers: God Stories*. It is an eminently priestly and pastoral work and, as such, it speaks as if in answer to the prayers offered up by all conscientious pastors of the flock ahead of undertaking the weighty privilege of preaching. The language is personal and warm; the style is theological and practical; the topics are scriptural and topical, addressing matters private and public, and relating the faith of Jesus Christ to the situations in which we all seek faithfully to live out our calling as sons and daughters of Christ.

The sermons selected for inclusion in this volume are, as one might expect from a cathedral precentor, profoundly devotional. They take their inspiration from, draw deeply upon, and are most properly understood within, the context of God's people at prayer. The Church's feasts and fasts are central, as is the rich sacramental heritage of the Anglican tradition and the broader tradition of English-language literature. The chapter headings themselves speak to this great breadth of influence and piety.

What has been produced here is a true labour of love, born of experience and wisdom, and flowing from a deep devotion to Jesus Christ, his people, and the world of his creation. May this fine work be to the community of St Peter's Cathedral, Adelaide, now celebrating over 150 years of faithful ministry, and to all who read it, a most profound blessing.

Christopher Stoltz
Westminster Abbey
Candlemas 2019

Preface

I first saw the photograph of the kingfisher on the front cover of this book in an exhibition of photographs in the South Australian Museum.[1] It seemed to me to be an image of God, and so I reflected on it in a sermon I gave in St Peter's Cathedral in Adelaide. Is this what preachers do? Do preachers say to the people sitting before them in church, "Maybe God is like this?" Preachers wrestle with the texts of scripture offered for the day of their sermon using all the intellectual tools that they can muster in mining the texts for some insight into God. Preachers stand in solidarity with those who sit before them struggling with the events taking place nearby in the local community or far away across the world. And after all this wrestling, isn't this what preachers do . . . pointing to an image or a story or a paradox . . . do preachers wonder with their congregations, "Is it possible that God is like this? That living as a child of God might be like this?"

When I arrived on my first parish placement in my formation for the priesthood, the parish priest gave my family a box of chocolates and gave me a book. *Under the Unpredictable Plant* by Eugene Peterson was my companion and guide throughout that time. This book told me who I was and what I was meant for:

> "What pastors do, or at least are called to do, is really quite simple. We say the word God accurately, so that congregations of Christians can stay in touch with the basic realities of their existence, so they know what is going on. We say the Name personally alongside our parishioners in the actual circumstances of their lives, so they will recognise and respond to the God who is both on our side and at our side when it doesn't seem like it and we don't feel like it. Why do we have such a difficult time keeping this focus? Why are we so easily distracted?"[2]

v

That is what I was for, simply, to "say the word God". Eugene Peterson is right, though, it is easy to get distracted. And one way to get distracted is to fall into the terrible trap that preachers can fall into and that is to try to control God's blessing of the congregation before us by telling people what to do, instructing them on how to live their lives.

Walter Brueggemann, that wonderful Old Testament scholar who writes so passionately about preaching, put it this way: "People are changed not by ethical urging but by transformed imagination."[3]

Walter Brueggemann describes the challenge of the preacher's task in one sentence! The preacher is to trust that God will speak to us through our imaginations, will guide us through our engagement with stories. This book is a collection of some of my attempts at preaching, inspired by Brueggemann's words.

I am sincerely grateful to many who have helped in the publication of this book. Heartfelt thanks go to Richard Hilton and Natalie Watson from Sacristy Press, for their faith in this book. Without two women from the congregation of St Peter's Cathedral, Di Nicholls OAM and Kathy Teague, this book would not have been written. Di and Kathy read nearly four years' worth of my sermons, chose sermons for the book, and together we ordered them, reordered them and gave them titles. Di, Kathy, Dr Rodney Fopp, Canon Bill Goodes, John Hamilton and my sister, Sara Wilson made up the editing team in Adelaide. My sincere thanks go to the Minor Canon and Precentor of Westminster Abbey, Christopher Stolz for his most generous Foreword and encouragement. Finally, I am most grateful for the support of the Dean of St Peter's Cathedral, Frank Nelson, and our fellow clergy and staff.

This book is dedicated to my husband, Nicholas, our two daughters, Lucy and Harriet, and to the people of St Peter's Cathedral in Adelaide, South Australia, for whom these sermons were written.

Jenny Wilson
St Peter's Cathedral, Adelaide, South Australia
August 2019

Contents

Foreword iii
Preface v

On Praying 1
1. Keeping Watch for Kingfishers 3
2. Sitting with the Truth 8
3. Spending Time with God 12
4. Keep Lighting Candles 17

Novels—Windows on the Soul 21
5. Grace through Goodness—*Middlemarch* 23
6. Showing Mercy—*The Grapes of Wrath* 27
7. Finding Hope—*Bleak House* 31
8. Walking in Our Shoes—*To Kill a Mockingbird* 36

Jesus' Encounters 41
9. They Have No Wine 43
10. Transforming the World 47
11. Cleansing our Planet 51
12. Tell It Slant 55
13. Do Not Be Afraid 60
14. Meeting God in Suffering 64

Saints and Festivals 69
15. "What Passing-Bells?"—Anzac Centenary 71
16. Beside a Fire of Coals—St Peter's Day 75
17. Pondering Joy and Pain—Mary 79
18. Nurturing the Soul—Music Sunday 82

Coming Home—In the Gospel of Luke 87
19. Anointing by the Spirit 89
20. Healing as Homecoming. 93
21. Sharing in God's Embrace. 97
22. Do Anything to Get Home 102
23. Heading Home 106

The Jesus Narrative 111
24. Whisperings of Poets and Prophets. 113
25. I'll ride with you. 117
26. Nativity—A Story Hanging in the Air. 122
27. Space for Our Souls 126
28. Behold the Wood of the Cross 130
29. Was it watching Notre Dame burn?. 135
30. Doubts and Loves Dig Up the World 139
31. Turning to Christ 143
32. A Loving Community 147
33. Bringing All Creation Home 151

Dates and Texts of Sermons 155
Notes 157

PART 1

On Praying

CHAPTER 1

Keeping Watch for Kingfishers

Today, I think, we might talk about prayer and the one in whose company we pray. We might spend a little time reflecting on how we imagine this God who creates us, redeems us, sanctifies us and seems to want to keep company with us. We might spend a little time imagining how it is that we pray in this God's company. For the scriptures give us some images this morning—the prophet Jeremiah speaks of God as a potter moulding his pot from clay, and that most intimate of Psalms, Psalm 139, writes of a creator who knows each of us so well that it is as if he knit us in our mother's womb. Images of God, not always comforting, though. Jeremiah's potter is portrayed working at his wheel and the vessel he was making of clay has been spoiled, and so that potter reworks the clay into another vessel, as seems good to him (Jeremiah 18:3–4). God, it seems, is not always pleased with God's creation. God doesn't walk away, though. God engages, and engages, always ready to remould us if we, as clay, will allow that remoulding to take place. God seems to be a persevering God.

I saw this, last week, when I stumbled across an image of God in a photograph.

Our South Australian Museum has on display an exhibition of photographs from a nature photography competition organized by the museum and *Australian Geographic*. As often happens, one photograph particularly caught my eye. This photograph seemed to remind me of God. The photograph, entitled "Hunting in the Rain", shows a kingfisher, drenched through, holding a centipede in its mouth. The photographer, Ofer Levy, wrote the following:

> I was in my hide photographing a pair of buff-breasted paradise kingfishers bringing food for their hungry nestlings. During the

five days I photographed them they didn't stop bringing food, even in the pouring monsoon rain.[4]

In this photograph, the kingfisher is standing on a large damp log, its bright eyes looking out, its beak determinedly clinging on to the centipede that will feed its young. The kingfisher looks so wet. This determined love, persevering loyalty, this searching for food in the driving rain, seemed to me to be a window into God who will not give up on us whatever the circumstances in which we, and so God, find ourselves.

It is the photographer, though, that gives us a glimpse of what the life of prayer might be like. That photographer was in his hide watching the kingfishers for five days. In the pouring monsoon rain.

Is that what prayer is? Keeping watch. Whatever the circumstances. Is that what prayer is like? Determinedly keeping watch?

The poet Ann Lewin wrote about prayer in this way. She might have known our photographer.

> Prayer is like watching for the
> Kingfisher.
> All you can do is
> Be there where he is like to appear, and
> Wait.
>
> Often nothing happens;
> There is space, silence and
> Expectancy.
> No visible signs, only the
> Knowledge that he's been there
> And may come again.
> Seeing or not seeing cease to matter,
> You have been prepared
> But when you've almost stopped
> Expecting it, a flash of brightness
> Gives encouragement.[5]

Seeing or not seeing cease to matter, this poet writes. The life of prayer is not about achievement, not about some measurable God response. It is about trusting what the psalmist says and giving God quite simply the gift of our time. Trusting what the psalmist says as he speaks with God:

> O Lord, you have searched me and known me:
> You know when I sit down and when I rise up;
>   you discern my thoughts from far away.
> You search out my path and my lying down,
>   and are acquainted with all my ways.
>
> *Psalm 139:1–2*

Whatever we sense of God's presence in our waiting, whether we see or we don't see, the image of God from this psalm is of a God who searches us out, who sees all that we do, knows all our thoughts and is acquainted with all our ways. And knew us, even before we knew ourselves.

We might wish to question this psalmist, though. For sometimes it doesn't seem that God is close. And sometimes we might ask ourselves if this God is safe? Do we dare keep watch in the presence of such insight, of such deep knowledge of us and all we are and all we know we can be? And what of Jeremiah's potter who broke the pot and began again?

The prophet Jeremiah is writing to the people of Israel in exile, when they are not unlike a pot which has been smashed to pieces. They are far away from home, from their land, their place of worship, the king that led them. All has been destroyed. In this strange land of exile, this remnant of the people of God finds that they are not abandoned. The prophet speaks of God as a potter who will rework them, will restore them if they will only turn to him.

"Turn now, all of you from your evil way, and amend your ways and your doings," God pleads to his people Israel in the final verse of our Old Testament reading this morning (Jeremiah 18:11).

The prophet Jeremiah does not hold back his words. The people of God in exile are just like a pot that has been smashed to pieces. The people will resonate with this description of their plight, and so they will hear the hope found in the image of the potter that will change his mind. They will find hope in Jeremiah's description of a God who will break and destroy and yet who will rebuild if the people turn away from their sins. An image of God who will rework the clay, who will form the pot again.

It is the prophet Isaiah, though, who speaks the words of turning, the words of the people of God begging God for restoration, using the images of potter and clay:

> Yet, O Lord, you are our Father;
> we are the clay, and you are our potter;
> we are all the work of your hand.
> Do not be exceedingly angry, O Lord,
> and do not remember iniquity for ever.
> Now consider, we are all your people.
>
> *Isaiah 64:8-9*

The Old Testament scholar Walter Brueggemann writes of Isaiah's prayer and of the image of God as potter:

> In this prayer it is not denied that Israel the clay has been recalcitrant to the will of the potter. Nonetheless, in the end, this clay does belong to the potter; this people does belong to this God; this child does belong to this Father. So the clay seeks forgiveness—seeks to have Yahweh the potter . . . move beyond anger in response to the needy pot. . . . In the end . . . Israel bids one last time that Yahweh will act as the potter did at the outset, to make wholeness possible again.[6]

What matters is that God has not gone away. This image of potter and clay holds a great truth, images a great closeness between God and God's creation. God waits. The one who longs for us to turn and pray is always listening for our voices, looking out for our approach on the horizon. When the prophets and the psalmist write these words, craft our conversation for us, the ground of all this writing is the presence of God. The abiding determined presence of God—the God who moulds us, knowing that circumstances, and sometimes our own sin, will smash us to pieces like a broken vessel. The God who waits for our cry that he might restore us again.

God waits, and works for our restoration with a determined love. Love like that of the kingfisher persistently bringing food to its hungry nestlings, in whatever circumstances.

And if God is waiting, perhaps the life of prayer is about waiting too. And so we might be encouraged to view the life of prayer as not unlike the life of the photographer who, in his hide for five days, kept watch for those kingfishers. In the pouring monsoon rain.

CHAPTER 2

Sitting with the Truth

There is a side chapel in York Minster which has a notice on its heavy wooden door saying, "This chapel is a place for prayer". Morning Prayer is, I suspect, said in this chapel, and the small weekday Eucharists are celebrated there. I've only been to York Minster a few times, but each time I've sat in that chapel and looked at the cross on the small altar. The steps into this side chapel are worn, like the steps in many churches and cathedrals in England, a sign that people have prayed in this place for hundreds and hundreds of years, and that we are welcome to join them there. I sat in that chapel and looked at the cross and thought of those I love, my family, my friends, the cathedral community in which I live and work, and that cathedral community's choir. And as I sat, I heard that choir sing. They were rehearsing a carol for Evensong which was to take place shortly, the carol which I think of as the "Lady Carol". Its true name is "The Shepherd's Carol", and its music was composed by Bob Chilcott. For me, it is one of the many lovely anthems that our choir sings. As I sat in that side chapel in York Minster, and I heard our choir sing the "Lady Carol", I wondered if this is what heaven would be like. A chapel with old worn steps, a place of prayer for many, many people and our beloved choir singing the "Lady Carol".

The shepherds are singing to Mary about their journey to visit her son. And there, at that stable, in that carol, they dedicate their lives to the baby they have come to worship.

"Our loves, our hopes, ourselves," these shepherds say, sing, "we give to your son."

This is what little side chapels with worn steps in great old English cathedrals, and churches old and modern, and our dearly loved cathedral and, in fact, the Jerusalem temple in the time of Jesus, are for.

The dedication of our loves, our hopes, ourselves to Mary's, *Lady's*, Son. The dedication of our hopes, our lives, ourselves, to that Son's Father, God.

And that is why Jesus raged when, as an adult, he entered the temple in Jerusalem and found it resembling a marketplace. The story is told in the second chapter of John's Gospel:

> In the temple [Jesus] found people selling cattle, sheep, and doves, and the money-changers seated at their tables. Making a whip of cords, he drove all of them out of the temple, both the sheep and the cattle. He also poured out the coins of the money-changers and overturned their tables. He told those who were selling the doves, "Take these things out of here! Stop making my Father's house a market-place!"
>
> John 2:14-16

Jesus knew, deep in his heart, what prayer was. Prayer defined him. His close relationship with his Father, whom he called "Abba", was at the heart of who he was. It may well have been, though, that, as it is for us, even for Jesus, prayer was not an easy thing. This may have been part of the reason why he was so angry that day when he entered the Jerusalem temple as an adult and why it was so devastating for him that that place of prayer was desecrated. Because Jesus knew that, as we find prayer a struggle, we are easily distracted by the things of the marketplace.

Prayer is not easy, because prayer, I believe, is sitting with the truth of our lives. Karl Rahner, a twentieth-century German Catholic theologian, wrote about prayer in the following way:

> When we are feeling lonely—if we are brave enough to resist the urge to call someone up, or go shopping, or take a drug, or turn to music or TV or go to bed; if we are courageous enough to remain alone and instead of fleeing the pain, to go down into it, we will gradually notice another Presence there, silent, but benevolent and peaceful.[7]

Karl Rahner is talking about not running away from the truth. And he is right to say that this takes courage. Sitting with the truth—be it the pain about which Rahner writes, or the fact that we feel trapped in a situation, or some disappointment, or a vague sense that we lack gratitude, be the truth even joy—sitting with the truth takes courage and we would often do anything to avoid it. Rahner knows human nature well when he catalogues the things that we will turn to in order to avoid sitting with the truth. If we are brave enough to resist those things, we may be brave enough to pray. Prayer takes courage.

Then Rahner suggests that we will find something in that place where we sit with the truth. He says that we will "gradually notice another Presence there, silent, but benevolent and peaceful". The presence of God. A presence that is usually known gradually, silently.

Christ's longing for us is that we know that presence, his Father's presence. He climbed mountains to be with God. But he also knew the temple as the place of prayer and the study of the scriptures, the word of God. It was his longing as he walked into the Jerusalem temple that day, as told in the Gospel of John, that God's presence be known. That is why he raged at those who tried to distract others from the difficult task of prayer. The difficult task of prayer in ordinary life. Like shepherds on the hills.

> We stood on the hills, Lady,
> Our day's work done,
> Watching the frosted meadows
> That winter had won.
>
> Oh, a voice from the sky, Lady,
> It seemed to us then
> Telling of God being born
> In the world of men.
>
> And so we have come, Lady,
> Our day's work done,
> Our love, our hopes, ourselves,
> We give to your son.[8]

That is what the Jerusalem temple was for and why Jesus raged—for the hearing of God being born in our world, for the giving of our lives. This is what temples and churches and our beloved cathedral are for. The hearing of the rumour of God, the gradual noticing of that silent benevolent presence. And that we might pray, at the end of the day:

> And so we have come, Lady,
> Our day's work done,
> Our love, our hopes, ourselves,
> We give to your son.

CHAPTER 3

Spending Time with God

The scene is the Last Supper. In John's account of this final meal that Jesus shares with his disciples, the key action is not the institution of the Eucharist, the giving of bread and wine. The key action is Jesus washing his disciples' feet. Jesus shows his disciples what his way of loving looks like, and then he gives his commandment to those washed disciples to love one another. The trouble is that they are beginning to realize that he will not be with them.

Jesus loves in many different ways in his life on earth and in this poignant scene before he leaves the disciples, his second key way of loving is through speech. Jesus talks and talks, in John's version of the supper, urging the disciples that their hearts not be troubled, and then describing to them what life in his and the Father's love looks like. Jesus teaches them with word and image. In John 15, Jesus uses the image of the vine. This image would be one that was familiar to the disciples in two ways. They would see vines about them, and they would hear of vines in their stories of faith. The image of the vine was deeply significant in the Jewish faith; Israel is the vine, God the vine-grower. "I am the vine, you are the branches. [Jesus says to his disciples.] Those who abide in me and I in them bear much fruit, because apart from me you can do nothing" (John 15:5). Jesus is the vine, and the Father, God, is the gardener.

Jesus speaks of pruning the vine and, apparently, the Greek word used in the text can mean cleansing as well as cutting. If that is the case, the image of the vine is immediately connected to Jesus' actions at the supper, of washing his disciples' feet. The consummate teacher, Jesus weaves his actions and his images, building a picture for the disciples of what their life in him, in God, is like. The disciples are to abide in him as he abides in God, and Jesus loves them by washing their feet, by pruning them as branches, preparing them for joy, for thriving and bearing fruit. Bearing fruit, an image that obviously relates to the image of the vine, means loving. "Love one another as I have loved you," Jesus says. "Bear fruit," Jesus says (v. 12). It's all the same thing. If we abide in Jesus in God's love, if we are washed and pruned by him, we will learn to love like him.

There is one more thing that Jesus says in the passage we heard read this morning that is worthy of our attention. We might think that it was our decision to live our lives in this faith in Christ; we might think that we have chosen him, but Jesus makes it clear that the choosing works the other way around. "You did not choose me, but I chose you," he says (John 15:16). We might think that Jesus approves of us, chooses us, if you like, on a good day, perhaps, when we have done some good deed or not behaved too selfishly. But that is not what Jesus is saying. Jesus chooses us, all of us, the heart of us. Jesus chooses us, and our families, our communities, and our world in this time and place with all its blessings and struggles. With all the things of which we are ashamed, Jesus chooses us, washes our feet and then bids us love one another.

One way of loving is to pray. Jesus' whole life was lived out of his deep praying life in his Father. He climbed mountains to pray. He gathered with others in homes and synagogues to pray. And bidden by his disciples, he gave us a prayer that is the essence of his prayer, a prayer we name after him. "Our Father in heaven," he bids us pray, "Hallowed be thy name, Thy kingdom come..."

The Archbishop of Canterbury, Justin Welby, has invited Anglicans across the world to join him in praying the prayer, "Thy Kingdom Come" from Ascension to Pentecost, and in our cathedral we are going to join him. We will celebrate the Feast of the Ascension this Thursday at a Eucharist at 7.30 in the morning and at a beautiful Choral Eucharist at 6.30 p.m. at night. We have videoed a number of us saying the words "Thy Kingdom Come" in different languages, and on Pentecost Sunday, in two weeks' time, we will hear all those languages spoken as we remember the story in the Acts of the Apostles when the Spirit came, when the disciples spoke about God's actions in Christ and when people from many different countries understood the things they said.

What is this kingdom, though? What does it look like? For what are we praying?

In Mark's Gospel, Jesus bursts upon the scene in Galilee, after his time of temptation and soul-searching in the wilderness saying, "The time is fulfilled, and the kingdom of God has come near; repent and believe in the good news" (Mark 1:15). Jesus clearly believes that in his life and ministry the kingdom is coming near, and that the way to engage with the kingdom is through repentance and faith. "Has come near" is an interesting phrase. We might think that Jesus would announce that the kingdom is *here*. But he does not say that. The kingdom is not yet here. But it is close by.

Before we look a little more closely at Jesus' words about the kingdom it will be helpful to reflect on the word "kingdom". Our image of it might be unhelpful. The word for kingdom in Greek is *basileia*. Scholars tell us that the word *basileia* would be better translated "reign"—that what Jesus is bringing in is the "reign of God". A kingdom for us might conjure up the idea of a place, a piece of land and a group of people that is owned and controlled and fought over. The kingdom of God is not like this—instead, it is about a way of living that is inspired by and guided by God. The words of the prophet Micah are well known and seem to hint at this reign of God:

> What does the Lord require of you
> but to do justice, and to love kindness,
> and to walk humbly with your God?
>
> *Micah 6:8*

Jesus knows that the reign of God that his presence is bringing near is difficult to understand, and so he teaches those with him about it in different ways. He tells us that we must receive the kingdom as a little child—with the openness and vulnerability and trust that children bring. He meets a rich young man who is searching for God and says after his meeting with the man, "It is easier for a camel to go through the eye of a needle than for someone who is rich to enter the kingdom of God" (Mark 10:25). The kingdom is indeed difficult to understand and so Jesus uses many parables to describe it. One of my favourite kingdom parables is about the mustard seed:

> With what can we compare the kingdom of God, or what parable will we use for it? It is like a mustard seed, which, when sown upon the ground, is the smallest of all the seeds on earth; yet when it is sown it grows up and becomes the greatest of all shrubs, and puts forth large branches, so that the birds of the air can make nests in its shade.
>
> Mark 4:30-2

What is fascinating about this image is that Jesus does not say that the kingdom is like a great shrub with large branches in which the birds might make their nests. He does not say that at all. He says that the kingdom is like a seed. A seed that is hidden in the ground, waiting. A seed full of potential for life and thriving but not seen. This is what the kingdom is like. And we can be greatly encouraged by that. For let us imagine a patch of soil with no seed in it, a barren patch of soil. Is there any hope in this image? And then, let us imagine that patch of soil with one mustard seed in it. Imagine the difference. Image the hope when there is just one mustard seed in a patch of soil waiting to grow, waiting for the rain and the warmth. Imagine the hope for life to emerge. And that gives us a little insight into what the kingdom of God is like. It is here, and yet we may not see it. It is present and waiting, and yet it is unseen. The kingdom may be like this and so we are encouraged to pray for that kingdom to come. "Thy kingdom come" we pray, and we will pray with Anglicans across the world from Ascension until Pentecost.

We will each pray this prayer differently. Who we are and what we care about matter as we pray for the coming of the kingdom. In chapter 10 of Mark's Gospel we read that Jesus asked Blind Bartimaeus, "What do you want me to do for you?" (Mark 10:51). This is one of the most important questions in the spiritual life. What do we want God to do for us? And when we pray for the coming of God's kingdom, we might ask the same question. "What do we most want God to do?" The answer to this question will become our prayer. It may be that we long that a dear friend knows that they are loved and forgiven by God. It may be that our great hope is for peace in a particular place in the world. It may be that we hope that no young person will sleep on the streets ever again. It may be that we grieve over the plight of our planet. For each one of us, our heart's desire will be different, but that desire will lead us to a way to pray for the coming of God's kingdom.

"You did not choose me, but I chose you," Jesus said. "Love one another as I have loved you." May we, each one of us, spend a little time in the days from Ascension to Pentecost knowing the love of God in Christ and praying in that love that God's kingdom may come.

CHAPTER 4

Keep Lighting Candles

In a speech during his time as President, after one of the many mass shootings in America, Barack Obama looked at the cameras and spoke almost in despair asking why he found himself speaking to his country about mass carnage again and again, saying he did not want to do that ever again. I could not find the text of that speech but his words to the press after the violence in Oregon in 2015 had a similar theme. "Somehow this has become routine," he said. "The reporting is routine, my response here at this podium ends up being routine, conversation after the aftermath of it . . . we have become numb to this." Preachers and people of faith across the globe might be asking the same question. Are our words, are our prayers, becoming routine? I could search through my files and "copy and paste" to write this sermon. "A man walked into a Lindt Cafe in Sydney and took hostage a group of innocent women and men and killed two of them." . . . December 2014. "A man walked into a Brussels airport and, blowing himself up, killed scores of people and injured many more." . . . April 2016.

And now . . . "a man walked into a Manchester concert venue" . . . A man walked into a Manchester concert venue and, blowing himself up, killed scores of innocent human beings and injured many more. And mothers and fathers across Britain and further afield leapt onto their phones to check that their loved one, their daughter, their son, was safe. I know that, because I was one of those mothers. We were saying Morning Prayer at clergy conference, and when we prayed for the victims of an attack in England and the city was not named, I jumped onto my phone to check that my daughter who is living in Exeter was safe. Only very quickly, after the relief, the guilt sets in because we know that for another mother, for many mothers and fathers, their loved ones are not

17

safe anymore. Like Barack Obama we may plead to God, how many more . . . and wonder if there is anything to say . . . and wonder if we might not better sit in silence in the face of this.

Only preachers, at least, cannot sit in silence. For this awful violence, and the love and the anger and the guilt and the feeling of utter helplessness that follows from such violence, are held. Held in a story. And our hope lies in remembering that story.

We know it, don't we? It goes a little like this . . .

A man walks into Jerusalem . . . Well he rides in, actually, doesn't he? A man rides into Jerusalem on a donkey, and the crowd waves palm branches and cries hosannas to herald his coming. But they got more than they bargained for, didn't they? He walks into the temple, and rages at those selling things there, that they have made his Father's house a robbers' den. That man lived and healed and loved and died out of his love for the one he called Abba, his Father, God. The relationship of closeness with God sustained him and gave him such courage and clarity about what he was to do. He gave many of those who he encountered freedom, but, when the religious leaders betrayed that God, he confronted them with their betrayal, with their sin.

When the time for the Passover comes, this man, Jesus, eats supper with his disciples and tells them what is going to happen and, when Peter says he will go with him, he says that he cannot go with him. And then, in John's Gospel, Jesus speaks for three chapters about how the disciples must not let their hearts be troubled, about his life of closeness to his Father, and he speaks about how the disciples are to abide in that love, how we are to abide in that love.

And then Jesus prays. The whole of chapter 17 of the Gospel according to John shows Jesus praying to his Father before he goes to his passion and death. Our Gospel reading this morning is part of that prayer. His prayer to God is for his disciples. Jesus' prayer shows his concern, not for himself, but for his disciples, and so for us, that we may know eternal life, life in God. He says:

> Father, the hour has come; glorify your Son so that the Son may glorify you, since you have given him authority over all people, to give eternal life to all whom you have given him. And this is

eternal life, that they may know you, the only true God, and Jesus Christ whom you have sent.

John 17:1–3

In John's Gospel, the glory is about Jesus' crucifixion and resurrection. Jesus knows what he is to face. And his great longing, his profound prayer, is that those he loves will be caught up in the life and love of God, might know eternal life, as he names it. This is not about life going on for all time in our time and place. But it is about a life that even death will not bring to an end. It is about a life of depth, a life held in God, a life struggling to know that it *is* held in God, a life of the wonder and challenge of prayer. Jesus prays, really, that we might pray.

And then he walked into the trap that hatred and sin set for him and he silently endured his trial and passion and died loving and forgiving those who put him to death. And God did glorify him, to use the language of John's Gospel. God set him free from death and in his resurrection he encountered and forgave and set free from fear those disciples who had cowered and run away when he needed them most.

And so here we are wondering about how we might pray for those caught up in violence in Manchester in England and for those killed by suicide bombers in Jakarta just a day later and for all the other things on our hearts. We might well want to say to God what the disciples said to Jesus in our reading from the first chapter of the Acts of the Apostles this morning: the disciples were gathered with the resurrected Jesus and they said to him, "Lord, is this the time when you will restore the kingdom to Israel?" (Acts 1:6). In other words, are you going to sort everything out now? In Barack Obama's words, we don't ever want to have to pray about this violence again, will you please sort it all out now? Jesus did not answer the disciples' question. He simply left them in the strange event that we call the ascension telling them to wait for the Holy Spirit. It seems that we are to try to find ways to keep on praying, to keep on trying to glimpse what it is to live in this eternal life that Jesus begs God to give us. It seems that we are to keep on praying.

A number of years ago I lit a candle each week for a close friend who was in a time of terrible struggle. I was in training at St Chad's in Fullarton, and I told the priest about my friend and about my lighting candles to pray for them. "What should I do?" I said, as it seemed that nothing was doing any good for my friend. "What else can I do?" ... "Keep lighting candles," he said. "Just keep lighting candles."

Each week in our cathedral as part of Choral Evensong on Wednesday nights at 5.30 p.m., we light candles for peace in the world. Last week we prayed the prayer written by the Church of England for the victims of the attack in Manchester, and we shall pray that prayer again this week.

A man walked into our cathedral during that candle-lighting service of Choral Evensong. The service was well under way, and the man joined us. But during the organ voluntary at the end of the service, the man came forward and lit a candle, and placed his candle in the bowl with the many other lighted candles, and he took a photo of the bowl and the prayer for the Manchester victims. He came over to me at the side door, and he shook my hand, and he said this: "I am the director of the Cathedral in Manchester. I will send this photo to my Dean. Please tell your Dean. Thank you for doing this."

Week by week, during school term, we gather on Wednesday evenings for Choral Evensong, and we light candles for peace. We would love to see any who wish to join us perhaps once a month or once in a while. Week by week we bring our helplessness and our anger and our guilt and our love for our fellow human beings across the world who are caught up in acts of violence. We might care for Manchester, because there is something there or someone there or a culture there that we can relate to. Our hearts are not as big as God's heart, after all, the God who loves and gathers in all who die in acts of violence and grieves for the world in which such violence takes place. God understands that our hearts are a little smaller than God's heart, though it is good if we remember that, I guess. It is good that we remember that we cannot care for all who need care.

Over and over again we gather in this cathedral to pray in the wake of senseless violence and the awful grief and fear it engenders. Strangely this does seem to be about a routine, perhaps we might call it a pattern, a pattern of prayer.

We struggle to pray, to dwell in a routine utterly different from the one Barack Obama grieved over, a routine or pattern grounded in the great love of God. A pattern we see in the life and death and resurrection of Christ. The life of prayer. The eternal life of prayer.

Keep lighting candles, I think. Let us keep on lighting candles.

PART 2

Novels—Windows on the Soul

CHAPTER 5

Grace through Goodness—*Middlemarch*

> What does the Lord require of you
> but to do justice, and to love kindness,
> and to walk humbly with your God?
>
> *Micah 6:8*

What does the Lord require? What is it to live the life that many of us long to live, a life that we might characterize as one of grace and goodness? A life that we might find imaged in the life of Christ, that one who came to dwell among us "full of grace and truth". What does the Lord require? We struggle with the question as we, understandably, feel that we so often fall short of it.

George Eliot, in her novel *Middlemarch*, explores the life of a town, Middlemarch, set in provincial England in the early part of the nineteenth century. The novel involves a rich tapestry of characters, at its heart focusing on two: Dorothea Brooke, who lives near Middlemarch under the guardianship of her uncle, and Tertius Lydgate, a doctor who comes to work in the town as the novel opens. George Eliot's portrayal of these characters involves two portrayals of defeated aspiration. They both long to have lives characterized by grace and goodness, to leave some reforming, blessing legacy. Both fail. Dorothea who longs to do some great good in the world finds herself naively caught in a marriage with a sterile and pedantic clergyman, Casaubon, who sees nothing of her hopes and dies crippled with an unjust jealousy of her friendship with his cousin, Will Ladislaw. Lydgate, who hopes to combine the reform of medical practice with research, is trapped in a life-denying marriage and a community fiercely resistant to new ideas.

We might wonder how a reflection on these characters is to inspire us, but inspire us they can as certainly, at times in our lives, they are us. We all long to do good, and at times we all fail. The reality and demands of ordinary life at times confine us. We find ourselves trapped by sickness or the frailty that comes with aging; we find ourselves in a workplace or life of retirement that seems mundane; we find ourselves simply not as bright, not as strong, not as wise as we once dreamed we might be. George Eliot's characters struggle in their longing to make some contribution of significance, a contribution that, on the surface of things, they seem to fail to make. I would like us to spend some time looking at George Eliot's reflections at the opening and close of *Middlemarch*. The novel opens with some thoughts on the life of Saint Theresa:

> Theresa's passionate nature demanded an epic life. Her flame... fed from within soared after some illimitable satisfaction, some object which would never justify weariness, which would satisfy self despair with a rapturous consciousness of life beyond self. She found her epos in the reform of a religious order...

Saint Theresa found her epos, her life's great work. George Eliot's own key characters, Dorothea Brooke and Tertius Lydgate, dream of such a life, such a work. And yet they are defeated. The reader of *Middlemarch* is prepared to encounter such defeat right at the beginning of the book in the final words of the Prelude:

> Here and there a cygnet is reared uneasily among the ducklings in the brown pond, and never finds the stream in fellowship with its own oary-footed kind. Here and there is born a Saint Theresa, foundress of nothing, whose loving heart-beats and sobs after an unattained goodness tremble off and are dispersed among hindrances, instead of centring in some long-recognizable deed.

After these words we are introduced to Dorothea, whose story will be summed up in these words from the Prelude.

So why spend time with this? Why encourage you to read or reread one of my favourite novels, a novel that seems to have at its core a story of disappointment? There are two reasons. One is that our founding story, the heart of our faith, the story of Christ, is a story of a defeat, a story of one who lived his life full of grace and truth and who died as a result of it. We must not rush from Jesus' death to his resurrection. For his death contains all our deaths, all our disappointments. Dorothea and Dr Lydgate are held there. Our lives are created and held in the love of God, the love of the Father and his Son in the power of the Holy Spirit. Death is part of it, at the centre of it, and only through death does resurrection come. Only through defeat does redemption come.

The second reason to spend time with this book, this evening in the middle of Lent, is the gift of *Middlemarch*'s writer, George Eliot, a gift given in her conclusion, a chapter entitled *Finale*. In this chapter, the author sums up the lives of her characters in order that the reader may say farewell. Dr Lydgate, she tells the reader, dies early, viewing his life a disappointment. Dorothea, though released from a marriage that imprisoned her and entering a marriage that was more life-giving, is described as always having felt "that there was always something better which she might have done, if only she had been better and known better".

Both live a disappointment. Both live in some way a defeat. Both, perhaps, remind us of ourselves, or someone we love dearly, who feels "that there was always something better which [they] might have done, if only [they] had been better and known better."

George Eliot does not leave her reader with her characters' pronouncement of disappointment on their lives. Disappointment does not have the final say. She writes a little more of her daughter in literature, Dorothea:

> Her finely touched spirit had still its fine issues, though they were not widely visible. Her full nature, [like a river] ... spent its time in channels which had no great name on earth. But the effect of her being on those around her was incalculably diffusive: for the growing good of the world is partly dependent on unhistoric acts; and that things are not so ill with you and me as they might have been, is half owing to the number who lived faithfully a hidden life, and rest in unvisited tombs.

This is the key; this is the hope. This is redemption, really. George Eliot names it. This is where grace and goodness touch the world—in the lives of ordinary people. For each one of us, for those we love. This is why God sent Jesus, the incarnate one, to live a human life. Grace and goodness are found in un-historic acts, in ordinary lives, in the day-by-day struggle of ordinary people living as best they can, who when they die are remembered by a few who loved them and were blessed by them. That is where grace and goodness are found.

CHAPTER 6

Showing Mercy—*The Grapes of Wrath*

> Have mercy on me, O God, according to your steadfast love;
> according to your abundant mercy blot out my transgressions.
> Wash me thoroughly from my iniquity,
> and cleanse me from my sin.
>
> *Psalm 51:1-2*

The story is told that King David wrote the words of this psalm, Psalm 51. He wrote them as he begged the forgiveness of God for a terrible sin. David coveted and took for himself Bathsheba, the wife of Uriah the Hittite, and, in order to keep Bathsheba for himself, he arranged that Uriah be placed "in the forefront of the hardest fighting . . . so that he might be struck down and die" (2 Samuel 11:15). David broke the Ten Commandments, the law given by God to help the Israelite people live well with God and with one another. David committed a terrible sin and Nathan the prophet revealed it to him. "Why have you despised the word of the Lord to do what is evil in his sight?" Nathan challenged the King (2 Samuel 12:9). And so David, challenged by Nathan and punished by the death of his and Bathsheba's child, poured out his repentance to God, repentance for his sin.

David's was a straightforward sin, a breaking of God's law by one human being. This sin was only redeemed by the repentance of that human being in the presence of God. Not all sin, not all evil is so straightforward. Not all sin, not all evil is so easy to pin down, to locate. Some evil, some sin is woven into the life of human institutions. And it is this evil, this sin, that we will explore as we spend a little time with John Steinbeck's novel *The Grapes of Wrath*.

Set in America during the Depression, the novel focuses on the Joads, a family of tenant farmers who were turned out of their Oklahoma home by drought, economic hardship, agricultural industry changes and bank foreclosures which forced them off the land which had given them their livelihood. The Joads set out for California where they hoped to find work. Their journey is narrated in the novel.

We've got a bad thing made by human beings, all right, but where does the bad thing, where does the sin lie? In this scene in which the tenant farmer and the tractor driver wrestle with locating the place of blame for the destruction of the farmer's way of life, we are given insight into institutional sin. Where does the sin lie? Who should the tenant farmer shoot before he starves: the one who gave the tractor driver his orders or the president of the bank? Or isn't it people at all?

And we are well aware that this type of sin, this institutional sin, is not confined to the Depression in America early in the twentieth century. Where is the sin located today in humanity's struggle in the care for our planet, where in the global community's wrestling with how to care adequately for those innocently displaced from their homes? Where are the sins of the twentieth century, and our century, the sins that modern warfare made possible, the sins we would not have believed humanity could commit? Where does that sin lie?

The theologian Walter Wink explores the idea of power for good or evil residing in an institution. In his book, *Engaging the Powers*, he writes:

> My thesis is that what people in the Bible called "Principalities and Powers" was in fact real. They were discerning the actual spirituality at the centre of the political, economic, and cultural institutions of their day. . . . the spirituality of an institution exists as a real aspect of the institution even when it is not perceived as such. Institutions have an actual spiritual ethos, and we neglect this aspect of institutional life at our peril.[9]

Walter Wink raises our awareness of the idea that an institution has, in some sense, a spiritual life, that good or evil can be found there not easily connected to individual human beings. John Steinbeck powerfully points to the difficulty that ordinary individuals like the Joad family have in locating the evil of an organization that is destroying their livelihood. "Who can we shoot?" the tenant farmer cried, when it is an organization that is to blame. Wherein does the guilt lie?

This understanding, this insight given by a snippet of a scene from *The Grapes of Wrath* and by the ideas of Walter Wink is not given that we might wash our hands of human responsibility for such institutional sin. The reverse is the case. Walter Wink goes on to write:

> Human misery is caused by institutions, but these institutions are maintained by human beings. We are made evil by our institutions, yes; but our institutions are also made evil by us. Not all sin can be projected outside the self; it is within us as well . . .

In the end, human beings are responsible. But an awareness of the institutionalized nature of sin can give us insight into the depth of the struggle we have in finding redemption in our world.

A whisper of that redemption is found in *The Grapes of Wrath* in the course of the book and particularly in its final chapter, when the reader witnesses characters who are profoundly vulnerable offering care to one another. Part-way through *The Grapes of Wrath*, we find the Joad family meeting up with another family, the Wilsons. Pa Joad invites Mr Wilson and his wife Sairy, who is dangerously ill, to travel with them to California. Sairy worries, though. Won't they be a burden? The Joads deny this. They will not be a burden. They will travel together. And, if they each help one another, they will all get to California.

If they each help one another, they will all get to California. If they each help one another. Therein is redemption found. In individual human beings reaching out in compassion to one another. That is where redemption is found.

And all redemption is found in the life and death and resurrection of one other human being. In the life and death and resurrection of Christ. The one who allowed the evil inherent in humanity to put him on trial, and place on his head a crown of thorns, and put on his back a purple robe; the one who allowed the evil inherent in humanity to put him to death, death on a cross.

Through Christ, redemption is found in God, the one to whom we cry for forgiveness for the individual and corporate sins in which we play our part. A cry so beautifully expressed in the words of David's psalm, Psalm 51:

> Have mercy on me, O God, according to your steadfast love;
> according to your abundant mercy blot out my transgressions.
>
> *Miserere mei, Deus: secundum magnam misericordiam tuam.*

CHAPTER 7

Finding Hope—*Bleak House*

Our theme this Lenten Evensong is justice, and a close reading of the Law and the Prophets in the Old Testament will leave the reader in little doubt as to the desire of God for justice, justice particularly for those who are in need. We hear, for example, the voice of God in the words of the prophet Isaiah:

> Is not this the fast that I choose:
> to loose the bonds of injustice,
> to undo the thongs of the yoke,
> to let the oppressed go free,
> and to break every yoke?
> Is it not to share your bread with the hungry,
> and bring the homeless poor into your house;
> when you see the naked, to cover them,
> and not to hide yourself from your own kin?
>
> *Isaiah 58:6–7*

Continuing our explorations of God themes found in novels, we will spend time with the novel *Bleak House* by Charles Dickens.

Bleak House is a novel in which Dickens cries out about the state of England. The novel opens simply with the word "London". And then the author goes on to describe the whole city as it is found in miserable November.

> Implacable November weather. As much mud in the streets as if the waters had but newly retired from the face of the earth . . . Fog everywhere. Fog up the river where it flows among green aits

and meadows; fog down the river, where it rolls defiled among the tiers of shipping, and the waterside pollutions of the great (and dirty) city ... Fog in the eyes and throats of ancient Greenwich pensioners, wheezing by the firesides of their wards ...

The circumstances are bleak in Dickens' description of his England—bleak for the environs and bleak indeed for the inhabitants. And in his novel, through the writing of his two narrators, he wrestles with the reason why things in England are in such a sorry and unjust state. One narrator is anonymous; the other, one Esther Summerson, is a young woman who believes herself to be without parents, who was raised by her aunt, who told her that she was her mother's disgrace and had better not have been born. We know what that means. Those who love Dickens will know well that his characters' names often reveal much, and *Bleak House* is populated with many such characters—Krook, Smallweed, Guppy, Sir Leicester and Lady Dedlock. The narrator, Esther Summerson—whose first name means star—will have some light to shine in the bleak wintry circumstances of the novel, despite her sad childhood.

Bleak House has as its centre a court case—*Jarndyce vs Jarndyce*. This case revolves around a will or series of wills. The case has gone on for years—generations even—drawing into its tentacles many who place their hopes on its conclusion in their favour. Esther enters the novel as a chaperone to one of the two wards of court in the case—Miss Ada Clare and Mr Richard Carstone. The three young adults are invited to live at Bleak House under the care of an older man, Mr John Jarndyce, one of the few characters who determinedly resists the case's clutches. Richard is not so strong of will. His hope that the case will afford him justice, in the form of riches, so possesses him that he cannot settle to any profession. Not even his great love for his fellow ward of court and cousin, Ada, or the wise counsel of Esther and Mr Jarndyce, can save him. Those who would profit from his entanglement in the case, among others a lawyer Mr Vholes, take over his time, his mind, his money and eventually his health. Richard dies, or "begins another world" as Dickens puts it, near the conclusion of the novel. A recently discovered will names Richard and Ada the beneficiaries, but it is revealed in court that all the proceeds have been consumed by legal costs. Who is to blame? Who is at fault for the wicked waste of time and life that the case *Jarndyce vs Jarndyce* caused for so many who entered the Court of Chancery? Wasn't everyone who worked on it just doing their job?

Two of the many other tragic deaths in the novel *Bleak House* were those of Esther's parents. Esther was born out of wedlock to a woman who was told by her sister that her child was dead. Keeping the story of her child a secret, the woman married a Lord, Lord Dedlock, (note the name) and lived with him at Chesney Wold, a country house that was *always* enfolded in rain. Lady Dedlock, described at one point in the novel as "in the desolation of boredom and the clutch of great despair", is always bored, always at the point of utter misery. The lie that is her life is in no way lightened by the gentle love and care of the husband whose name and title she has taken. When she recognizes the handwriting of her lover on a legal document brought by the family lawyer, Mr Tulkinghorn, she risks exposure of her story through that lawyer to follow the trail of that handwriting. The lover, known in the early stages of the novel as Nemo—which means no-one—has died from an overdose of opium by the time she finds him. A crossing sweeper boy, Jo, who was treated kindly by Nemo, leads her to his pauper's grave.

As the novel reaches its conclusion, Esther, who by now has met her mother, is seen searching frantically for her. Sir Leicester Dedlock has been told of his wife's illegitimate child by those who would gain money in the story's telling. Lady Dedlock flees, after writing to him begging his forgiveness—"I have no home left," she writes, "I will encumber you no more. May you in your just resentment be able to forgive the unworthy woman on whom you have wasted a most generous devotion—who avoids you only with a deeper shame than that with which she hurries from herself—and who writes this last adieu". After a long search—one of the many fruitless searches in the novel—Esther finds her mother dead at the iron gate that leads to her lover's burial place. The reader knows that Lord Dedlock would have forgiven her; Esther wants only to love her. The reader wrings their hand at the wasted lives of characters they have come to love. So who is to blame? Where does the injustice lie for this sad thread of the story? The moral code that could not allow the restoration of one who has borne an illegitimate child?

We will make note of one more of the many deaths in this tale . . . that of Jo, the crossing sweeper boy. For it is in the telling of this death that Charles Dickens cries out in a way that might remind us of Jesus, crying out over Jerusalem. Jo is an orphan who walks the streets and sweeps the crossing near the court of chancery. "Name Jo. Nothing else that he knows of. No father, no mother, no friends. Never been to school. What's home? Knows a broom's a broom and knows it's wicked to tell a lie . . . ". Jo contracts smallpox in Tom-all-Alone's where he sleeps at night with others who are destitute and, through a series of circumstances, finds himself cared for by Esther who also catches the disease. After a struggle, Esther survives though her beauty does not. As Jo lies dying back in London, his longing is to beg her forgiveness. Jo dies, forgiven, with the three characters of hope in the novel *Bleak House* at his side, whispering the Lord's Prayer. Esther, Mr Jarndyce and Alan Woodcourt, a doctor who works alongside the poor and who loves Esther despite her disfigurement, sit with Jo as he enters peace for the first time. The author, though, is not at peace. Almost seeming to step out from behind the guise of the narrator through which he usually speaks, Dickens openly laments the unjust circumstances of his character Jo's death.

> "Dead. Dead, your majesty. Dead, my lords and gentlemen. Dead, Right Reverends and Wrong Reverends of every order. Dead, men and women, born with heavenly compassion in your hearts. And dying thus around us, every day."

Again, who is to blame? Who is guilty of Jo's death? And who, even more, is guilty of the poverty of Jo's life?

The English scholar, Terry Eagleton, writes the following in the preface to the 2003 edition of *Bleak House*:

> To see what is awry with the world as bred by a whole system represents an unusual insight on Dickens' part. In his earlier fiction you could usually pin the blame on a stage villain like Fagin, Dombey or Uriah Heep . . . If the system is at fault, then no one individual can set it to rights; if nobody is responsible, then, as Esther believes, we all must be.[10]

As Esther believes ... Esther and Mr Jarndyce and the doctor Alan Woodcourt all believe ... that they all have a part to play in "loosing the bonds of injustice", as the prophet Isaiah put it.

And we might wonder, if Charles Dickens was writing today, about what systems he might write, against what injustices he might rail—climate change, financial crises on a global scale—or perhaps the injustices that seem to remain the same in our time as they were in the time in which he was writing: poverty, the effects of being captured in the processes of the law and the moral codes of our time that so often offer little opportunity for forgiveness.

Somehow in their actions in this novel, Dickens' characters, Esther Summerson, Alan Woodcourt and Mr John Jarndyce represent a different spirit from that bleak spirit which is so aptly represented by fog in the novel. Their spirit of hope and their longing for a just world does not prevent the many pointless deaths in the novel. But it does, like the author's voice, rail against them, lament them and work against them; the dogged hard work of those who hope to bring love into the world and often seem to fail—the spirit of hope that we might believe finds its origin in God.

CHAPTER 8

Walking in Our Shoes—*To Kill a Mockingbird*

In this series of sermons we have been spending time with some of my favourite novels, finding there some ideas about God. One of my favourite novels is *To Kill a Mockingbird* by Harper Lee. Set in the sleepy Alabama town of Maycomb at the time of the Great Depression, the story of *To Kill a Mockingbird* revolves around a trial, in which a black man is wrongly accused of raping a white girl. The story is narrated by Scout, aged eight, who lives with her brother Jem and their widowed father Atticus. It is Atticus who will defend Tom Robinson, the man accused of rape.

Early in the novel, Scout comes home from school raging about the injustices meted out by her teacher, Miss Caroline. Scout and Miss Caroline's first day at school has not gone well. Scout, a prolific reader, has arrived at school, where her teacher, Miss Caroline, has instructed Scout that her father, Atticus, is not to teach her anymore, as it will interfere with her reading. This is not the limit of Miss Caroline's misdemeanours. At lunchtime Miss Caroline accuses one of her students, Walter Cunningham, of forgetting his lunch. In his embarrassment, Walter lies in response. Walter has not forgotten his lunch; he never had any lunch. When Miss Caroline tries to give him a quarter and tries to insist that Walter accept it, Scout tries to intervene. Surely it is enough to tell her new teacher that Walter is a Cunningham? Everyone else in the classroom knows that the Cunninghams don't have money for lunch.

Arriving home, Scout has decided that she won't go to school any more if it is alright with Atticus. He asks what the matter is. Gradually she tells him about the day's misfortunes. She tells him about Miss Caroline telling her that Atticus is not to teach her to read any more. She tells him about

Miss Caroline not knowing that you don't give lunch money to Walter Cunningham, because he will never be able to pay it back. Atticus thinks for a while and then he says to Scout that you never really understand a person until you consider things from their point of view . . . until you climb into their skin and walk around in it . . . until you put yourself in their shoes.

Atticus' plea to Scout is woven through layer after layer of this wonderful book. You never really understand a person until you consider things from their point of view . . . until you climb into their skin and walk around in it. Don't judge the black man, Tom Robinson, who is on trial; don't judge the hidden neighbour Boo Radley, of whom you are terrified, because all you know of him is the frightening stories people have told; don't judge Mrs Dubose, the grumpy old lady across the road, and don't even judge your teacher. Every strangeness has a story. Don't judge a person until you've stood in their shoes.

This theme is writ large at the close of the first part of the novel, in one of its most poignant moments. Jem and Scout are struggling with the response of many of the inhabitants of Maycomb to the news that their father is defending the "Negro", Tom Robinson. Neighbours, relatives and school students frequently refer to Atticus as "nigger lover". Atticus implores Jem and Scout not to respond, but when their cantankerous neighbour Mrs Dubose calls out that Atticus was "in the court house lawing for niggers!" Jem goes to her home and breaks off every camellia bush Mrs Dubose owns, until the ground is covered with buds and leaves from the plants she loves. When he arrives home that night, Atticus sends Jem to see Mrs Dubose and talks to Scout about the trial that lies ahead. He must act for Tom Robinson, he says. His conscience demands it.

Jem returns from seeing Mrs Dubose and announces that she wishes him to read to her every day for a month. So Jem and Scout visit Mrs Dubose, and Jem reads to her, every day for a month and then for another week. Mrs Dubose is very ill in bed as Jem reads to her, and towards the end of the reading time she has strange fits. Then the alarm on her clock rings, and they are allowed to leave. A month after the reading sessions have come to an end, Atticus answers a phone call and announces that he is going to visit Mrs Dubose. When he returns, he tells Jem and Scout that Mrs Dubose has died. He tells Jem that Mrs Dubose was addicted to morphine and that, before she died, she wanted to break her addiction. That was why Atticus had made Jem read to her, to help distract her through the struggle to break her addiction.

And then Atticus hands Jem a box from Mrs Dubose. In the box is a perfect white camellia. His arms around the sobbing Jem, Atticus tells him that he wanted him to see that their cantankerous difficult neighbour was a great lady, one of the most courageous people he had ever known.

It is true. You never really understand a person until you consider things from their point of view . . . until you climb into their skin and walk around in it.

And so, thanks to Atticus, Jem climbed into the skin of an old lady dying and determined, before she died, to break an addiction to morphine.

In Part Two of *To Kill a Mockingbird*, the story is told of the trial of Tom Robinson. Despite Atticus discrediting Bob Ewell, the father of the allegedly raped girl, Tom is convicted of rape, and he is shot as he tries to escape from prison. Bob Ewell vows revenge on Atticus. Bob Ewell attacks Jem and Scout while they walk home on a dark night after the school Halloween pageant. Jem's arm is broken during the struggle, but amid the confusion someone rescues the children. A stranger. The strange rescuer carries Jem home, and after a little while, Scout realizes that the person who saved their lives is Boo Radley.

Boo Radley is perhaps the most seriously misjudged character in the novel. For until this moment at the close of the novel, Boo Radley is not seen. And if we haven't seen someone what can we do but believe the stories that are told about them? As the novel closes, Scout summarizes the plot from Boo's viewpoint, as she leads Boo home after he has saved their lives. She concludes as she stands on the Radleys' front porch looking out over Maycomb Street, a view she has not seen before, that Atticus was right . . . that you can never really know a person until you have walked in their shoes.

So where is God in this? What has all this to do with God?

Well, that is just what God did, you see . . . just what God did in the incarnation, if you want to use a technical religious term. God climbed into our skins and walked around in them. The Word became flesh and dwelt among us full of grace and truth, as John's Gospel says. God embraced our point of view. God was born on this earth and lived a human life and God died a human death. And so we know, as we prepare to walk with him this Holy Week, that the one who created us and redeemed us has walked in our shoes.

PART 3

Jesus' Encounters

CHAPTER 9

They Have No Wine

"They have no wine."

Wine symbolizes life.

"The life source is gone." The source of life, of joy, of exuberance, has dried up, is finished. "They have no wine."

It is Mary, Jesus' mother, who points this out to him. The story of her giving birth to him is not told in John's Gospel, which begins instead well before Jesus' birth, at creation's birth. But Jesus' mother gives birth to his first sign. She invites him to notice and respond to this terrible lack, this lack of wine at a wedding, and in so doing she invites him to begin his revelation of who he is and, more importantly, who God is.

Mary appears twice in this Gospel, at the wedding at Cana and at Jesus' death. She is present at the moment when he restores life to a wedding feast and at the moment when blood and water stream from his pierced dead side, pouring life and spirit into creation.

John's Gospel is woven with symbolism, and this story of the wedding at Cana is no exception. Before we look more closely at the story we have read, we need to think a little about the opening and closing scenes from the Gospel.

John's Gospel opens before the dawn of time, with a prologue that echoes the Genesis account of creation. It gives the ground upon which the whole Gospel story is told:

> In the beginning was the Word, and the Word was with God, and the Word was God. . . . What has come into being in him, [Jesus], was life, and the life was the light of all people. The light shines in the darkness, and the darkness did not overcome it . . .

> And the Word became flesh and lived among us, and we have seen his glory, the glory as of a father's only son, full of grace and truth.
>
> *John 1:1,3–5,14*

Jesus, the Word of God, came and lived among us, that we might have life, that we might become children of God. Jesus came, that God's glory might be revealed.

And, importantly for our passage, very near the end of the Gospel, the writer tells us the reason for his writing:

> Now Jesus did many other signs in the presence of his disciples, which are not written in this book. But these are written so that you may come to believe that Jesus is the Messiah, the Son of God, and that through believing you may have life in his name.
>
> *John 20:30–1*

The Gospel is written that we might believe . . . and have life in his name, that we might believe and have life. So let us look more closely now at this wedding scene, the scene where Jesus performed his first sign. A sign points beyond itself to something. It nurtures the question, "What is happening here?" It causes us to wonder.

The scene opens with the words "on the third day". These words would have an immediate resonance with hearers familiar with the Old Testament. When Moses has led the Israelite people into the wilderness, in one encounter with the Lord:

> The Lord said to Moses: "Go to the people and consecrate them today and tomorrow. Have them wash their clothes and prepare for the third day, because on the third day the Lord will come down upon Mount Sinai in the sight of all the people . . . "
>
> *Exodus 19:10–11*

The words "on the third day" would lead to an expectation that God is to be revealed in some way. We well remember that the ultimate revelation of God's glory, as John puts it, was revealed when Jesus was raised on the third day".

So the very opening of this story tells us that we might be open to the possibility of God. The setting of the story is a wedding feast. Again, in the writing of the Old Testament, God is at times portrayed as a bridegroom longing to be united with God's people Israel. The love of a marriage is a symbol of God's abiding love, of God's abiding longing to be deeply connected with God's people. And so we sense that God's desire to love God's people is at hand.

But there is a problem at this wedding. "They have no wine." The wine has run out. Wine is the source of joy and exuberance at a feast. The source of life has run out. Jesus, we remember from the prologue of John's Gospel, was life, lived among us that we might have life. The truth expressed in the beautiful poetry of the prologue is now to be enacted in this first sign. Jesus' mother is the one who notices what is happening and she goes immediately to her son and tells him.

His response is strange. "Woman, what concern is that to you and to me? My hour has not yet come." The scholar Michael Fallon suggests a different translation of these words, a translation that he believes is more faithful to the original text. He believes Jesus is saying to his mother, "Are you seeing this the way I see it? Woman, has not my hour now come?"[11] He seems to be inviting her to ponder how God wishes them to be involved in the situation. "Are you seeing this the way I see it?" Surely his mother does see the situation the way he sees it. She has come to him and her faith is palpable. She tells the servants to do whatever he tells them to do. Jesus' hour, in John's Gospel, is the time of the crucifixion, but Jesus is affirming that at this time, in this first sign, he is to begin to reveal who he is, and what he has come to do.

> Now standing there were six stone water-jars for the Jewish rites of purification, each holding twenty or thirty gallons. Jesus said to them, "Fill the jars with water."
>
> *John 2:6*

These water jars were probably for the ritual cleansing of hands at a meal. At the moment they are empty, waiting to be filled. In this turning of water into wine, Jesus creates something new in the midst of the Jewish culture.

In Jesus' hands the water becomes wine, good wine, in abundant supply. This is an extravagant action; it is profoundly generous. This wine is a gift of extraordinary grace.

The Gospel writer concludes his account:

> Jesus did this, the first of his signs, in Cana of Galilee, and revealed his glory; and his disciples believed in him.
>
> *John 2:11*

Jesus is indeed present, full of grace and truth, the truth being that where life and joy is lacking, Jesus brings both in abundance. The glory of God is revealed in this first sign, this sign that contains the key revelation—that of God's great love. And the disciples believed. Michael Fallon defines "believe" as "to be in God's love, receiving with an open heart the love which God is".[12]

"They have no wine." We could gaze at so many situations in our world and say those words. Sometimes we look at one another, in our families or our workplaces or our communities, and if we have the courage of Jesus' mother we might say: "*We* have no wine." Do we dare to speak her words, to see what she sees? Could we imagine Jesus saying to us "Are you seeing this the way I see it?" Is it a time to be in God's love, receiving with an open heart the love which God is? Can we believe, when the wine, the life source, seems to have run out? Can we, like Jesus' mother, go to him and see ourselves and the world in which we live the way he sees it?

A sign such as this causes us to wonder. What is Jesus doing here? Can it possibly be that here the great love of God is being revealed? Might we allow the words, "We have no wine" with all their pain, ring in the air, when life seems diminished; might we, like Jesus' mother, in faith, speak them out aloud? Might we allow the possibility that God in Jesus will hear us and will offer us abundant life?

CHAPTER 10

Transforming the World

You are the salt of the earth . . . he said.
You are the light of the world . . . he said.
He says, *You are here to transform the world.*
You. Us.

They are on a mountainside. In this section of Matthew's Gospel, known as the Sermon on the Mount, we see Jesus teaching his disciples, in the first of five passages of teaching in the Gospel. This year we are spending time with the Gospel of Matthew, a Gospel written particularly for Jewish hearers, a Gospel which portrays Jesus, not only as healer and prophet, but particularly as a teacher.

Mountains are God country. And the Jewish hearers of this Gospel could not have helped remembering Moses and his encounters with God on Mount Sinai. Only, when Moses spoke to the people he led into the wilderness from slavery in Egypt, Moses spoke of God in the third person: "The Lord said to me . . ." (Deuteronomy 10:1). "When you have come into the land the Lord is giving you . . ." (Deuteronomy 26:1). "The Lord your God is commanding you . . ." (Deuteronomy 26:16).

Jesus doesn't speak like that at all. Jesus just says "*I* say to you . . .", "Truly *I* say to you . . ." over and over again. This mountain is God country and Jesus is speaking in the first person, "I". This is a *very holy person* we are listening to here.

And this very holy person says to the disciples, and is saying to us: "You are the salt of the earth . . . You are the light of the world . . . You are here, in other words, to transform the world."

This is a weighty description of us. It is extraordinarily difficult to believe, and yet . . . wonderful. Can we believe this? That we are here to transform the world? We as individuals, we as community. We as country even, in a time when, God knows, we need God's voice to be heard.

When he has said these words, Jesus, knowing human nature, as he does, points to the disciples' and our struggle with this extraordinary vocation:

> You are the salt of the earth; but if salt has lost its taste, how can its saltiness be restored? It is no longer good for anything, but is thrown out and trampled under foot.
> You are the light of the world. A city built on a hill cannot be hidden. No one after lighting a lamp puts it under the bushel basket, but on the lampstand, and it gives light to all in the house. In the same way, let your light shine before others, so that they may see your good works and give glory to your Father in heaven.
> Matthew 5:13-16

Let us spend a little time pondering the struggle.

If we accept that we have this God-given vocation to be salt and light, what is it that causes salt to lose its taste, what is it that has us hide our light under bushel baskets? What is it that diminishes us so?

Fear, I think, is one of the key contenders. Sin, of course, is another. Jesus is a literary master, one who is very good with images, and "light hiding under a bushel basket" is an astute image of one who is fearful. What nurtures this fear? I wonder if fear may come from a broken imagination, our imagining that we might be who God has made us to be. Can we remember God calling us into a situation that frightened us greatly, as if we couldn't imagine ourselves there? Imaginations are damaged by circumstance. Some of us have experienced terrible suffering, in the form of violence or abuse. Such suffering damages in the most profound way our imagination about ourselves, what we believe about ourselves. Some of us are shaken by illness or grief. For some of us, home has become unsafe and we now live far from home. Imagining who we are away from the *earth* of our home, the community of our home, can diminish us. Some of us could not name why, but dis-ease about the call of God seems to haunt us.

Jesus knows this. The passage from Matthew 5 follows immediately on from the strange blessings called the Beatitudes. Jesus knows our struggles and has named them just before he tells us we are light and salt, just before he tells us we are to transform the world.

"Blessed are the poor in spirit, and those who mourn." Jesus says. "Blessed are the meek and those who hunger and thirst for righteousness. Blessed are the merciful, and the pure in heart, and the peacemakers and those who are persecuted for righteousness' sake."

This is not about being successful in the world's eyes; this is not about worldly power. Jesus is saying that we are blessed, that God is with us, close to us, when we are struggling. That it is precisely *there*, precisely where we might least think it possible, that we can bring blessing to the world.

Paul, in the First Letter to the Corinthians, says a similar thing:

> When I came to you, brothers and sisters, [he writes], I did not come proclaiming the mystery of God to you in lofty words or wisdom. For I decided to know nothing among you except Jesus Christ, and him crucified. And I came to you in weakness and in fear and in much trembling. My speech and my proclamation were not with plausible words of wisdom, but with a demonstration of the Spirit and of power, so that your faith might rest not on human wisdom but on the power of God.
>
> *1 Corinthians 2:1–5*

For Paul, the key thing that matters is Christ crucified. The moment of profound failure in Jesus' life is God's moment of redemption. In a culture in which we would expect Paul to convince his readers by eloquent argument, Paul does not do this, does not use lofty words or wisdom, as he puts it. He simply points to Christ on the cross as a sign of God's power and presence in the world.

The Beatitudes and Paul's writing point in different ways to the same truth. When we are struggling, when we seem in the midst of failure, God is with us, God is close; God's work of healing and redemption is at hand. Do not therefore be frightened to be salt, to be light, to be as individuals and communities engaged in God's transformation and healing of the world. Jesus is telling us not to allow our frailty to stop us standing on that hill as light to the world. That, in fact, it is precisely *when* we are frail, or frightened, that we might go to our hill and shine our light there.

What, though, would God have us do? What does salt and light look like? If we can find the courage, even at times, to be that salt and light, to what do these images point? The prophets are never backward in telling us what they think about this matter.

Here are some words given to us by Isaiah:

> Is not this the fast that I choose:
> to loose the bonds of injustice,
> to undo the thongs of the yoke,
> to let the oppressed go free,
> and to break every yoke?
> Is it not to share your bread with the hungry,
> and bring the homeless poor into your house;
> when you see the naked, to cover them,
> and not to hide yourself from your own kin?
> Then your light shall break forth like the dawn . . .
>
> *Isaiah 58:6–8*

Our light shall break forth like the dawn when we loose the bonds of injustice and let the oppressed go free. I wonder if this could be about forgiveness. Is there anyone we need to forgive, anyone whose forgiveness we need to seek out? Injustice and oppression have many guises. Our light shines forth when we share our bread with the hungry and cover the naked. Isaiah says.

Shining a light in the world, allowing our lives to transform the world, seems to be about knowing that we are blessed even in places of struggle and vulnerability, knowing we are blessed and allowing our imaginations to thrive there, knowing we are blessed and reaching out in forgiveness and generosity to those who are in need.

You are the salt of the earth . . . Jesus said.
You are the light of the world . . . he said.
He says, *You are here to transform the world.*

CHAPTER 11

Cleansing our Planet

A leper comes to Jesus, and kneeling he begs him, "If you choose, you can make me clean." Moved with pity, or compassion, or is it anger at the plight of the man, [as some translations of this passage in Mark's Gospel have it], and moved at the very depths of his being, Jesus stretches out his hand and touches the man with leprosy, and says to him, "I do choose. Be made clean!" And immediately the leprosy leaves him, and he is made clean (Mark 1:40–1).

The leper knows who Jesus is and calls out to him. Jesus sees his suffering, knows his pain, observes his exclusion, and he heals and restores and brings to life this child of God. This dynamic, the cry of the one who suffers and God's perpetual hearing of that cry, is woven into creation . . . woven, perhaps, not only for the struggle of individual human beings. The possibility of God's healing presence is also here for our planet.

David Attenborough, the naturalist and broadcaster who understands and loves so many things about our planet and has inspired many of us through his television series to love a little more his great love, made a TV series, *Blue Planet II*. Reflecting on that series, David Attenborough has spoken about the health of the planet and the bird and animal life with which we share our home. He speaks about the effect of plastics on the environment. "We've seen albatrosses come back with their belly full of food for their young and nothing in it. The albatross parent has been away for three weeks gathering stuff for her young and what comes out? What does she give her chick? You think it's going to be squid, but it's plastic. The chick is going to starve and die."[13]

One newspaper article further explored the theme: "Should you ever travel to one of the many uninhabited islands that dot the most remote reaches of Earth's oceans, chances are you'll find plastic bottles littering the shore. Even if there's nothing else to be found there, civilization's obsession with plastic waste is having a profound impact on every corner of the globe. One million plastic bottles are bought every minute around the globe, fuelled by our insatiable thirst for bottled water.

The annual sale of plastic bottles will soar to a staggering one trillion by the end of this decade—a twenty-per-cent increase. Most of those bottles end up in landfill, where they take a significant time to break down, or in the ocean. One scientific report . . . found the equivalent of a garbage truck worth of plastic bottles was being dumped into the ocean every minute. What this all means is an imminent environmental crisis that some experts predict could be just as dangerous as climate change."[14]

Each one of us has seen pictures in social and news media of whales with their stomachs choking in plastic bags, of birds with their stomachs filled with tiny and less than tiny pieces of coloured plastic that they are enticed into believing is food. We have seen photos of seashores covered with plastic bottles. What does God see as God looks upon our planet from the sky? A white film of plastic on the shores and seas that were to be a safe home for sea life, for human life? A white film of this substance that threatens to choke us . . . a white film not unlike leprosy, perhaps, on the planet?

Does the planet cry out to God: "If you choose, you can make me clean"?

A number of biblical scholars in Adelaide have developed what is known as *The Earth Bible Project*. This project involves reading the Bible from the perspective of the earth, viewing the earth as a subject in the biblical text, acknowledging that the earth may have a voice in the biblical text and listening for the cry of that voice, the wisdom of that voice and listening for God's response to it. We know from the creation account in Genesis that God created the earth and all the animals of the earth, the fish in the sea and the plants upon the earth, and that God views all these things as good, as very good. We know that God loves all that God has made.

Does the planet cry out to God: "If you choose, you can make me clean"?

And can we doubt that Jesus gazes on the planet with pity and compassion and raging anger at what has been done to her and replies: "I do choose, be made clean."

And yet ... God has no hands but ours. Didn't someone once say:

> Christ has no body now but yours. No hands, no feet on earth but yours. Yours are the eyes through which he looks with compassion on this world. Yours are the feet with which he walks to do good. Yours are the hands through which he blesses all the world. Yours are the hands, yours are the feet, yours are the eyes, you are his body. Christ has no body now on earth but yours.

A poet whispers as we wonder how Christ can heal our beautiful earth. But the problem is so vast, isn't it?

> Naaman, commander of the army of the king of Aram, was a great man ... [and] though a mighty warrior, [this great man] suffered from leprosy. Now the Arameans on one of their raids had taken a young girl captive from the land of Israel, and she served Naaman's wife. She said to her mistress, "If only my lord were with the prophet who is in Samaria! He would cure him of his leprosy."
>
> 2 Kings 5:1–3

Our earlier Old Testament reading was about Naaman, the army commander. It is fascinating to read the prophet Elisha's instructions to Naaman, that he might be healed of his leprosy. And the way in which this mighty army commander responded is even more fascinating. "Go, wash in the Jordan seven times, and your flesh shall be restored and you shall be clean," instructed Elisha. Naaman is offended that the prophet has not waved his hands over him crying out in the name of the Lord. Naaman's servants say to him, "Father, if the prophet had commanded you to do something difficult, would you not have done it? How much more, when all he said to you was, 'Wash, and be clean'?" So Naaman goes down and immerses himself seven times in the Jordan, according to the word of the man of God; and his flesh is restored like the flesh of a young boy, and he is clean (2 Kings 5:10–14).

It is interesting that Elisha the prophet did not even meet Naaman to help this healing to take place. Naaman was not asked to do some great and difficult thing but was asked to be vulnerable and to do a simple thing, a humble thing—to know himself powerless and yet to play his part.

Is that what God is asking of us? As we imagine the planet plagued with the leprosy that is plastic, is that what God is asking of us?

Does the planet cry out to God: "If you choose, you can make me clean"? Can we, like Naaman, know ourselves powerless and yet play our part?

David Attenborough said in an interview: "Plastic manufacturers happily say when you've used it throw it away, discard it. There is no away. Plastic is so permanent, so indestructible that when you've cast it into the ocean it does not go away. . . . I am certain that when people understand the consequences of what they are doing that they will care for the rest of the world in a profound way . . . There are simple things that we can do. . . ."[15]

There are simple things we can do, David Attenborough says in faith, sure that when we understand we will care in a profound way. Could we in our cathedral commit to supporting each other as we explore what simple things we could do to help care for our planet? Could our imagining of our future involve playing a small part in bringing about a healed planet?

In all these things we are not alone.

The man with leprosy in our Gospel reading sensed the presence of Jesus, and it was to Jesus, God's Son, that he cried out: "If you choose, you can make me clean."

And Jesus, moved with pity made his reply. His spirit is with us. If, as David Attenborough says, when we understand we will care in a profound way, that understanding, that care, that healing of how we see the needs of the planet will come from God. If, inspired by Naaman the Syrian, we can embrace our powerlessness and yet still play our part, that embrace, that action, will be blessed by God. May we pray with the leper, "If you choose, you can make us and our world clean". May we hear God's reply: "I do choose, be made clean."

CHAPTER 12

Tell It Slant

"I love you," says God . . . "let me say it again another way."

A priest I once knew was talking about God, imagining God having a conversation with us. And God saying, "I love you". And then realizing that we have not heard, or have not understood, or perhaps more importantly have not felt, God saying, "Let me say that again, another way". God longs that we will hear. Jesus, God's Son, longs that we would hear too.

In chapter 18 of Matthew's Gospel, Jesus says what he wishes to say one way, and then in another, and then yet in another way, such is *his* longing that we would know the ways of God. Matthew's Gospel, written for a Jewish audience, often portrays Jesus as a teacher. The Gospel has five passages of teaching, the first and most well-known being the Sermon on the Mount. Jesus, like Moses, ascends a mountain and then talks of God, beginning his words with the Beatitudes, those strange blessings that are so counter to the ways of the world. Chapter 18 is the fourth passage of teaching and contains two themes: the theme of who matters and the theme of how people are to relate to each other and, particularly, how people are to forgive in God's community. We will address the first theme here.

Jesus has been gathering and instructing a community of disciples in the midst of growing opposition from the religious leaders. As we heard last week, Jesus has told his disciples that following him involves them taking up their cross. Strange blessings, strange instructions. Jesus pauses again to teach the disciples and the teaching in Matthew 18 comes in response to a question. No doubt struggling with Jesus and his strange words, and struggling with the opposition of the religious leaders, the disciples ask the wrong question, if you like, or at least a question that shows they have absorbed little that Jesus has said.

"Who is the greatest in the kingdom of heaven?" they say. They are clearly not comfortable with the vulnerability of life with Jesus where beatitudes are to be followed and a cross is to be carried. Let's have a little power instead. Who is the greatest?

Jesus starts with a definition:

> He called a child, whom he puts among them, and said, "Truly I tell you, unless you change and become like children, you will never enter the kingdom of heaven. Whoever becomes humble like this child is the greatest in the kingdom of heaven. Whoever welcomes one such child in my name welcomes me."
>
> *Matthew 18:2-4*

The greatest in the kingdom of heaven is like a child. That is his definition. This is certainly not what the disciples would have expected, for children in Jesus' time and place were invisible. He was not being romantic about them; he would have known that children, like adults, can be winning on some days, and profoundly irritating on others. That is not the point. He is making the invisible visible, the ignored, noticed. To be great, you must be like the least, he is saying. This is about a radically different understanding of status. It is about abandoning self-reliance and the desire for power; about living in community in a place of trust in God.

Jesus then speaks about the issue of stumbling. It is a vivid idea. Stumbling happens when we are walking along a path, in this case the path of the kingdom of heaven, and something causes us to trip up, to be halted in our walking, our living well in the way of God. Jesus has come that we might thrive in the great love of God and that we might encourage one another in that way. But Jesus says:

> If any of you puts a stumbling-block before one of these little ones who believe in me, it would be better for you if a great millstone were fastened around your neck and you were drowned in the depth of the sea. Woe to the world because of stumbling-blocks!

> Occasions for stumbling are bound to come, but woe to the one by whom the stumbling-block comes!
>
> *Matthew 18:6–7*

We know that Jesus is not beyond using dramatic exaggeration to illustrate his point. Woe to us if we ever cause a "little one", a vulnerable member of our community to stumble, to be tripped up in the way of God. Woe to us if something about us causes us to stumble; it is better that that aspect of us be thrown away. The stumbling that Jesus is speaking about here relates to the context, to the question he has been asked: who is the greatest? The one who is like a child. If anything about you gets in the way of this, if anything about you encourages you to seek power, and especially power over the vulnerable, the "little ones", look carefully at it and let go of it:

"Who is the greatest in the kingdom of heaven?"

We are part of the way through Jesus' response. He is not interested in the idea of greatness. If you want to enter the kingdom at all, you must be like a child, he says. Jesus defines, and he uses dramatic exaggeration to give some insight into the way of God: to give insight into a kingdom where power and status cause stumbling, where power and status are not life-giving at all.

Jesus knows, though, that we find these things very difficult to understand and so he uses, finally, his best armoury, his greatest teaching tool. He tells a story.

Walter Brueggemann, the Old Testament scholar, wrote the following: "People are changed not by ethical urging but by transformed imagination."[16] Don't tell people what to do, in other words, tell them a story that will change how they see the world.

Rowan Williams, a theologian and former Archbishop of Canterbury, writes of God being represented by a whole narrative, a whole story particularly when Jesus speaks in parables.

Emily Dickinson says it in a poem:

> Tell all the truth but tell it slant –
> Success in Circuit lies
> Too bright for our infirm Delight

> The Truth's superb surprise
> As Lightning to the Children eased
> With explanation kind
> The Truth must dazzle gradually
> Or every man be blind –[17]

The truth must dazzle gradually—the truth of God will reach us rarely through instruction, rarely via definition. The truth will reach us perhaps through parable, through story: "Tell it slant . . . "

And so Jesus finishes his response to the question of the disciples with a parable and one we know well, the Parable of the Lost Sheep:

> What do you think? If a shepherd has a hundred sheep, and one of them has gone astray, does he not leave the ninety-nine on the mountains and go in search of the one that went astray? And if he finds it, truly I tell you, he rejoices over it more than over the ninety-nine that never went astray.
> *Matthew 18:12–14*

I have been told that the best thing to do with a parable is to let it irritate us. To discover what we do not understand. And this place of not understanding may well be different for each one of us, not surprising if we allow ourselves to be encountered by the living word of God. Is there anything irritating about this parable? We are so accustomed to it that it may be difficult to imagine the reaction of those hearing Jesus for the first time. Let us put ourselves in the place of each of the characters in the story. What must the shepherd be feeling to search out the one sheep who goes astray? What is the response of the ninety-nine sheep left behind? And what of the lost sheep? What does it feel like that the shepherd would risk the lives of all the others, that the shepherd would bother to go out on the mountains in search of him . . . of her? What is our response? What do we not understand? With whom do we most relate?

Jesus is telling God's truth *slant* here in this parable. And he is telling *all the truth*; he is not only telling us what God is like, but he is telling us what we are like too. Does this extravagantly loving shepherd annoy us? Does he seem simply irresponsible? Or do we remember when we were utterly lost. Are we utterly lost? And does this extraordinary love come to us as an incomprehensible and joyous relief?

Jesus tells God's truth in stories in the end. And who best hears, responds to, revels in stories?

"Truly I tell you," Jesus says, "unless you change and become like children, you will never enter the kingdom of heaven."

Children hear stories. Children revel in stories. Children allow themselves to be moved, to be transformed by stories.

Become like children, Jesus says, and then you will understand the ways of God. Then you will know how to thrive in the kingdom of heaven. Then you will hear God say that the lost ones are God's great loves and might be our great loves too, which is a great blessing, for we all know that on some days, at some times in our lives, those lost ones, those little ones are us. Strange kingdom this, that it is when we are humble and frail that we are thriving in the kingdom of heaven.

"I love you," says God. Searching across the mountains for God's sheep that is lost. "When I find you, I'll say that again another way."

CHAPTER 13

Do Not Be Afraid

"Do not be afraid," Jesus said.

The question is: why should we take his advice?

Jesus has just fed a large crowd, and he seems to need some time alone. Before he goes up a mountain by himself to pray, he encourages his disciples to get into a boat and set out on the sea. When evening comes, though, a storm arises and the boat, battered by the waves and the wind, is far from the land. Early in the morning, Jesus comes walking towards the disciples on the lake. But when they see him walking on the lake, they are terrified, crying out in fear, saying, "It is a ghost!" Immediately Jesus speaks to them and says, "Take heart, it is I; do not be afraid" (Matthew 14:22–7).

Jesus' whole life story is enclosed with these words: "Don't be afraid." The angel Gabriel speaks them to his mother, Mary, before Jesus' conception—"Do not be afraid for you have found favour with God"—and, at the end of Jesus' life story, angels speak to the disciples who come looking for Jesus' body at his tomb three days after his death, saying those same words: "Do not be afraid." Woven through the Old Testament, as well, the prophets repeatedly exhort the people of Israel to abandon fear. "Do not be afraid for I have redeemed you. I have called you by name. You are mine," God says through the prophet Isaiah in one of my very favourite passages in the prophet's writings, Isaiah 43.

Fear seems to be a key aspect of the human condition. God knows this, and God urges against it.

The boat in which the disciples are travelling is floundering on a stormy sea with the wind and the waves against them. We get this, don't we? Stormy seas and the fear that accompanies them. Human life is woven with this. Sickness does this; a serious illness can overwhelm and threaten to drown us. The death of a loved one does this, the death of one we cannot, perhaps years after their death, imagine that we must live without. The way of a world in which "terrorism" is a household word does this. Terrorism isn't about killing people, don't you see? Those two planes didn't fly into the Twin Towers in New York all those years ago to kill people. The lives lost were just collateral damage. The aim was to terrorize, to disrupt the lives of men, women and children by instilling fear of what can happen. The purpose was the image. The idea was a television image that would breed terror in us. And then there is this planet that is our home. Our home is under threat. We might well worry about how we can adequately care for it, especially when one world leader is trying to remove the words "climate change" from his country's vocabulary. We might, wisely, be frightened by that. Yes, we know about fear.

And the stormy sea with the winds and the waves and the little boat floundering on it is an image which gives much insight into fear. Insight into what seems to be our powerlessness in it.

In the Gospel story, though, this boat is not alone. Early in the morning Jesus comes walking towards the boat on the lake. It is very important when we engage with a scriptural text, with any text, that we understand its language, that we ask of it the right questions. As we know, from the opening verses of the creation account in Genesis, the sea, in biblical thought, represents the forces of chaos, those forces held at bay by God's creative power. And, again, in the narratives of the scriptures, it is only *God* that walks on the sea. Little wonder the disciples, who think Jesus is praying up a mountain, are further terrified by his presence. "Take heart, it is I; do not be afraid," Jesus says. "It is I" or "I am" is God language, is reminiscent of God saying "I am who I am" to Moses by the burning bush. God is present with the disciples in the boat on the stormy sea.

Before we begin to engage with Peter's response to Jesus, we need to ponder this presence. The whole of Matthew's Gospel is about this. We have said that the stories of Jesus' life begin and end with angels telling people not to be afraid. There is something beyond this, something which holds frightened humanity. A presence. Matthew's Gospel is bookended with the fact of this presence, surrounded by an assertion of it. In the opening chapter of the Gospel, an angel tells Joseph in a dream not to be afraid to take Mary as his wife, and the Gospel's narrator comments that her child will be named "Emmanuel, God with us" (Matthew 1:20–3). As the Gospel draws to a close, in the final verse, in fact, we see Jesus saying to his disciples "Remember, I am with you always, to the end of the age" (Matthew 28:20). If the writer of this Gospel would have us remember one thing it is that God is with us. That even, perhaps particularly, when we are afraid, God is with us. And the image of Jesus walking on a sea where the wind is howling and the waves are threatening to overturn any boat travelling upon that sea is a powerful sign of that presence. We would be wise to notice that Jesus does not seem to be bothered about the sea. It is the fear of his disciples that has engaged his attention.

Any text from scripture tells us something about God and something about what it is to be a human being. And if we can allow that story to sit alongside our human story, we can be transformed by it. God is with us, walking alongside us on our stormy seas. But how can that help us?

Rowan Williams in his book about language, *The Edge of Words*, writes about how Jesus and the writers of scripture use narrative, story, to help us engage with the idea, the possibility of God. He says, "God is represented by a whole narrative; to enter into this story and discover where you as a hearer fit and what role it is possible for you to adopt imaginatively, is to become able to offer a representation that claims truthfulness . . . ".[18] In other words, the truth about God is often too difficult to engage with as a definition or an assertion. If we were simply to say, "Everything will be OK because God is with us", we may find ourselves incredulous or unmoved. The truth about God, though, may be found in a story, may reach us through a story. And the truth of God in the presence of frightened humanity may be found here in the story of Peter and his response to Jesus' presence walking on the water.

The first thing Peter does is engage with Jesus. We know fear can render us incapable of response, but Peter's fear does not do this. The word courage has the word heart woven into it—he has literally *taken heart* as Jesus put it—as he tries to trust Jesus. Peter takes courage and names Jesus "Lord"; he says, "Lord, if it is you, command me to come to you on the water". And Jesus says, "Come". But the fear is not defeated. I guess we can all relate to what happens next.

Peter looks at Jesus, looks at the one who gives him courage as he sets out across the stormy sea—and then he changes the object of his gaze. When Jesus has bidden Peter follow him out onto the water, all of a sudden, all Peter can see is the wind and the waves, and he loses sight of Jesus standing just a little way away. And don't we know that feeling? When we step out in faith on an adventure we have longed to go on or we decide that we can embrace a struggle that we cannot seem to avoid, and then we find ourselves wondering what on earth we have taken on and how on earth we will manage it. Fear takes over.

But, again, when Peter notices the strong wind, becomes frightened, and begins to sink, he cries out, "Lord, save me!" Peter trusts Jesus just enough to call to him. Again, the fear does not freeze him into inaction. Peter prays. And Jesus immediately reaches out his hand and catches hold of Peter, saying to him, "You of little faith, why did you doubt?"

All through this, as the sea rages and the wind howls, Jesus and Peter engage, Jesus willing Peter to have faith—Peter longing to act in faith. Faith and fear and doubt and love are swirling in the midst of that terrifying sea. And, in the end, Jesus catches hold of Peter and both of them step into the boat; the wind ceases and the sea is calm (Matthew 14:28–33).

God is with us, do you see? There could just be the sea and the fear. That might be all there is. And some days it seems like all there is. But the whole of the biblical text and the whole of the life and death and resurrection of Jesus is saying that the sea and fear are not all there is.

And our part, like Peter, is to cry out, because even a frightened cry is an act of faith. That may be all we can manage at first. To cry out and to step out because the stories of scripture and the one to whom we will hold out our hands this morning for bread and wine are all about us trusting that it is just possible that we are not alone. That God is with us. And that living in that truth will calm the stormiest of seas. It will bring light and life in the darkest and most frightening places.

CHAPTER 14

Meeting God in Suffering

"What do you want me to do for you?" Jesus says to a blind man who has cried out twice, fighting his way through the disciples' disapproval, to get to him (Mark 10:46–52).

"What do you want me to do for you?" says the one who is the image of God, giving to that blind man such integrity that he might name for himself his healing.

In this, possibly my favourite of the healing stories, some fascinating things happen. Firstly, Bartimaeus cries out, and, when he is told by the disciples not to bother Jesus, he continues to cry out. In the scriptures there are several key themes—God themes. And one of these is the theme of exodus. In a sense every healing is an *exodus* story. Bartimaeus comes to Jesus *enslaved* by his blindness. In the story of the Exodus, God freed the people of Israel who were in slavery in Egypt. And God acted to free God's people *in response to their cry*. The Old Testament scholar Walter Brueggemann says that "It is of great importance that the initial impetus for the exodus confrontation was not from [God] but from the slaves who groan and cry out . . . It is Israel's cry that evokes [God]".[19] In every story of Jesus' healing we find a cry. It may be the cry of the one who is in need of healing, as in the case of Blind Bartimaeus; it may be the cry or the prayer of one who loves them. Every healing is in response to a cry. Somehow what God needs to heal is an expression of the truth. The truth of the pain of the illness whatever it may be; for Bartimaeus the truth of the pain of blindness and the diminished life this blindness causes.

The next aspect of the story is the strangeness of Jesus' response. "What do you want me to do for you?" Jesus says to the man born blind. This seems an extraordinary question. Jesus, who has deep insight into the needs of those with whom he keeps company, surely knows what this man needs. What integrity Jesus gives this blind man when he asks *him* to name what it is he longs for. Not only is his pain voiced but his heart's desire. Everything comes from within the blind man. Jesus' presence just helps him to speak the truth. And so Jesus names the source of the healing as the man's own faith. "Your faith has made you well." Immediately he regained his sight and followed him on the way. The statement of the man being made well happens *before* he gains his sight. It is as if the wellness is in the cry of the pain of blindness and the voicing of the desire for sight. For Jesus that is what it is to be well. The regaining of sight comes after.

Blind Bartimaeus trusted Jesus. And Jesus had compassion on him. Rowan Williams in his book, *Meeting God in Mark*, describes the healing found in Jesus' presence in this way:

> Trust heals people . . . Jesus' healings are always bound into a relation between him and the person to be healed. . . . Out of [the] meeting of trust and compassion comes the miracle.[20]

Only a miracle doesn't always come, does it? People aren't always healed, are they? We pray and pray for the ones we love, for ourselves, and sometimes the healing we long for doesn't seem to come. We find ourselves struggling with a debilitating disease; sometimes someone we love dearly dies. And sometimes injury, or even death, strike unexpectedly, and we didn't even know we needed to pray, to struggle to trust, to keep our loved ones safe. Was Jesus out of compassion that day? Wasn't our faith enough?

Job is another character in the scriptures who cries out to God. Job, whose story we conclude this week in our Old Testament reading, finds himself in a place of awful suffering, covered in sores, sitting on an ash heap. His friends sit with him for a little while but then their compassion runs out. His friends point out that Job must have committed some sin for which his suffering is the punishment. The friends, who kept company with Job for a time, desert him.

And so Job cries out to God. Job bewails the absence of God in his suffering. God has deserted Job—"if I go forward, he is not there," Job cries, "or backward, I cannot perceive him" (Job 23:8). Job begs God for vindication, for the opportunity to "lay [his] case before him" (Job 23:4). Finally, Job cries out, "let the Almighty answer me!" (Job 31:35).

Again we see a key character in the scriptures cry out to God.

In the final chapters of the book of Job, God answers Job. God answers Job "out of the whirlwind" (Job 38:1). God does not explain anything. God does not even engage with Job's questions. Instead, God bombards Job with question upon question, encounter upon encounter, leading Job to contemplate the mystery of creation. "Where were you when I laid the foundation of the earth? Tell me if you have understanding. Who determined its measurements—surely you know! Or who stretched the line upon it? On what were its bases sunk, or who laid its cornerstone when the morning stars sang together and all the heavenly beings shouted for joy?" (Job 38:4–7).

When God is finally silent, Job replies, in the reading we have heard this morning, "I know that you can do all things and that no purpose of yours can be thwarted . . . Hear and I will speak; I will question you, and you declare to me. I have heard of you by the hearing of the ear, but now my eye sees you; therefore I despise myself in dust and ashes" (Job 42:2,4–6).

What God gives Job is not an explanation but an encounter. The suffering of the innocent Job is not made comprehensible in any of God and Job's wrestling, but God gives God's presence, as Job gave Job's own. Like Blind Bartimaeus in his encounter with Jesus, Job poured out his truth to God and God honoured that outpouring. In the midst of suffering we see the relationship between Creator and the created one thriving. In the midst of acute suffering, Job experienced an encounter with God which transformed his relationship with God and transformed his life. Here in this wilderness, Job finds himself in worthy company after all. "I have heard of you by the hearing of the ear, but now my eye sees you", says Job.

We so long to be made well, when we are ill. We so long for our loved ones to be made well. The scholar John Pilch has made a study of the cultural significance of Jesus' healings in his book *Healing in the New Testament*.[21] He makes the key point that healing in our culture is about restoration to *functioning*, while healing in Jesus' time and place was about restoration to *community*. We long to be able to continue to do the things we do, to make the contribution we make. We long to be able to continue to function. And one of the key reasons for that is that we think our worth is found there. In Jesus' time a person's worth was found in their identity as members of a family, members of a religious community. Sickness often caused a person to be cast out from a community. Healing restored them to their place of belonging.

In both the story of Job and the story of Blind Bartimaeus, we see the one who is suffering cry out to God, bring their struggle and their longing for healing in prayer to God. And God hears, and God has compassion, and the God who made us and longs for us to live, gathers us in. And this may not be the healing we ask for. It may not look like what we imagined. But we will find ourselves encountered by and enfolded in the love of the one who will hold us even in death.

PART 4

Saints and Festivals

CHAPTER 15

"What Passing-Bells?"—Anzac Centenary

One hundred years ago, at dawn on 25 April 1915, a force of Australian and New Zealand soldiers, who came to be known as Anzacs, landed on the Gallipoli peninsula, playing their part in an Allied campaign to invade Turkey. This campaign ended in defeat about nine months later. Allied casualties numbered 141,000 with 44,000 dead. Turkish casualties were double this.

The World War I poet, Wilfred Owen, wrote an anthem in response to his experiences in the trenches of that war, his response, an offering to those who died there. Owen entitled his poem *Anthem for Doomed Youth*:

> What passing-bells for these who die as cattle?
> Only the monstrous anger of the guns.
> Only the stuttering rifles' rapid rattle
> Can patter out their hasty orisons.
> No mockeries now for them; no prayers nor bells;
> Nor any voice of mourning save the choirs,—
> The shrill, demented choirs of wailing shells;
> And bugles calling for them from sad shires.
>
> What candles may be held to speed them all?
> Not in the hands of boys but in their eyes
> Shall shine the holy glimmers of goodbyes.
> The pallor of girls' brows shall be their pall;
> Their flowers the tenderness of patient minds,
> And each slow dusk a drawing-down of blinds.

This morning, in our cathedral, we heard our choir sing a psalm that is often sung for those who, unlike many of those who died in war, *do* have funerals. This psalm, Psalm 23, is often sung or read, chosen to bring comfort to us as we mourn the one who is dead, to bring comfort as we ponder the truth that dying is something we will all face. The psalm of the good shepherd.

This morning we place this anthem and this psalm alongside one another. We need to be careful not to think that one overtakes the other, that the psalm of comfort somehow anaesthetizes the anthem, which is racked with pain. We need to be careful about this. For that is not what is happening here.

"The Lord is my shepherd, therefore can I lack nothing", the psalmist says. And a little further on: "Though I walk through the valley of the shadow of death, I will fear no evil, for you are with me, your rod and your staff comfort me."

We need to allow the *Anthem for Doomed Youth* and Psalm 23 to sit alongside each other, to resonate with each other, to be a truth one for the other, and in that resonance to listen for the voice of God, to know that we are not alone as we remember the horror that was war and that war still is.

"I am the good shepherd," Jesus says.

Our Gospel reading, from chapter 10 of John's Gospel, finds Jesus in conversation with the Pharisees. Jesus has just healed the man born blind and the religious leaders are trying to accuse him of acting sinfully. Far from acting sinfully, Jesus is saying that his actions show deep care for those whom he encounters. Jesus challenges the Pharisees with contrasting images of those who might have responsibility for the care of a flock of sheep. The image of the shepherd is contrasted with the image of the hired hand. There is little doubt with which image Jesus is comparing the Pharisees:

> The hired hand, who is not the shepherd and does not own the sheep, sees the wolf coming and leaves the sheep and runs away—and the wolf snatches them and scatters them. The hired hand runs away because a hired hand does not care for the sheep.
>
> *John 10:12–13*

The hired hand does not own the sheep and does not care for the sheep. And so, the minute there is any sign of danger, the hired hand runs away. While the hired hand's task is to look after the sheep, as there is no love for the sheep, the hired hand's first care is for himself. The good shepherd is different. His relationship with the sheep is different:

> The sheep hear his voice. He calls his own sheep by name and leads them out. When he has brought out all his own, he goes ahead of them, and the sheep follow him because they know his voice. They will not follow a stranger, but they will run from him because they do not know the voice of strangers.
>
> *John 10:3–5*

The relationship is about speaking and hearing. The good shepherd knows the sheep by name, and they know his voice. The relationship is about knowing and being known. And this closeness comes from the closeness of Jesus and the Father:

> I know my own and my own know me, just as the Father knows me and I know the Father.
>
> *John 10:14–15*

The sheep are drawn into this close relationship of love, a love that is so deep that the shepherd will give his life for his sheep. "I lay down my life for the sheep", Jesus says (John 10:15).

Jesus would have known that what he was saying would resonate with the image of the shepherd that so often appears in the scriptures of the Jewish people.

In Ezekiel 34, God says through the prophet:

> As shepherds seek out their flocks when they are among their scattered sheep, so I will seek out my sheep. I will rescue them from all the places to which they have been scattered on a day of clouds and thick darkness.
>
> *Ezekiel 34:12*

And then there is Psalm 23 in which the writer of the psalm describes a relationship of closeness and care with his God, imaged as shepherd, a God who will accompany us in all things, whose "goodness and loving-kindness will follow us all the days of our life", who will comfort and uphold us even as we walk through the valley of the shadow of death.

"I am the good shepherd," Jesus says.

In our cathedral this evening we will remember those who gave their lives in the Gallipoli campaign. We will hear readings from letters and diaries of those who took part in the campaign and from those who loved them dearly. The photo on the front cover of the service booklet for tonight shows a soldier carrying a fellow soldier. It is not clear if the fellow soldier is alive or dead. The Gallipoli peninsula is in the background. This photo seems to me to say something very significant about the valley of the shadow of death. It is said in the photo, and it is also said in Wilfred Owen's poem *Anthem for Doomed Youth*. When the soldier is carried by his fellow soldier, he is not alone. When Wilfred Owen writes so powerfully and so painfully about the deaths of his fellow soldiers, they are not alone. Although he describes a lonely and unacknowledged death, Wilfred Owen's poem acknowledges those deaths. He stands in solidarity with all those who have died in war. He witnesses to those who died.

Rowan Williams once alluded to the idea that the presence of God is about our being witnessed to, about our lives being witnessed to. We do not live unnoticed, we do not die unloved. And so when Jesus says that he will lay down his life for his sheep, what he says is true. He did lay down his life for his sheep. But this laying down of life is not a once-only thing. It is true that theologians will say Christ's dying was in some sense once and for all. But there is another way in which Jesus dies for us and that is in his being present with those who die, present in the arms of the soldier who carries his dead or wounded fellow soldier, present in the poet who has the courage to state the horror of those lonely and painful deaths.

"I know my own and my own know me," Jesus says.

That is what this Good Shepherd Sunday is all about. Jesus, present and holding us, in all the valleys of the shadow of death that we and all we love have known and will know, Jesus, present and holding those who died in war, and those poets who railed against the dying in war, Jesus present and holding all creation, all things, in death and in life.

CHAPTER 16

Beside a Fire of Coals—St Peter's Day

There is a determination in the voice of God as portrayed in our first reading from the book of the prophet Ezekiel:

> I myself will search for my sheep, and will seek them out. As shepherds seek out their flocks when they are among their scattered sheep, so I will seek out my sheep. I will rescue them from all the places to which they have been scattered on a day of clouds and thick darkness. . . . I will seek the lost, and I will bring back the strayed, and I will bind up the injured, and I will strengthen the weak, but the fat and the strong I will destroy.
>
> *Ezekiel 34:11–12,15–16*

I will, I will, I myself will, says God. I will search for my sheep, and seek them out, and seek them out again, even if I have to die in the attempt, and break through the bonds of death, and seek out the lost on the other side.

Which, of course, is exactly what Jesus did for our beloved, and so utterly flawed, patron saint, Peter. He died and broke through the bonds of death and sought out the lost on the other side.

Each weekday morning, in this cathedral dedicated to Saint Peter, we say prayers in the Dean's Chapel, just a few steps away from the sacristy. I sit looking towards the stained-glass windows, as we say our prayers, and there is a window there that we might dedicate to our patron saint. In the background of the window Jesus is bound and held by a group of soldiers. He looks with great sadness towards the foreground of the window. There, in the foreground, a servant girl is talking with a man who we know is Peter. The window doesn't show this, but the text from John's

Gospel tells us that Peter and the servant girl are warming themselves by a fire of coals. Right in the foreground of this stained-glass window is a bird, a cockerel. Jesus' face shows the pain of the betrayal that is taking place before his eyes. He knows what lies ahead of him, that he is to face an unjust trial and a painful death, and he knows that his best friend is too frightened to accompany him there. Three times Peter denies Jesus. Three times he says that he does not know him. And then the cock crows, as Jesus told Peter it would, and Peter dissolves in tears.

Sin is like that. We commit it out of fear, or weakness, or the desire for self-preservation. We commit it out of many other reasons as well—greed, pride, vanity, lust . . . But in Peter's case it was fear. We commit sin quickly and without thinking, hurriedly before we can reflect on what we are doing, we deny, betray, run from the good and courageous act we might do, and then . . . then the cock crows, and we remember Jesus' voice. We remember our prayers and our hopes and our promises to God that we would do our best . . . The cock crows and, like Peter, we weep for our weakness and wonder if we can ever look God in the face again.

The cock's crow, though, heralds the dawn, the coming of the light. It is here in John's Gospel, a Gospel that is all about light and darkness, that Peter, perhaps, first sees who he is and who Jesus is. Peter, knowing that Jesus has died, would have been wracked with guilt, sure that he would never have the opportunity to ask for forgiveness, sure that he would never look Jesus in the face again.

He does, though, have the chance to look Jesus in the face again. Jesus meets Peter and several of the other disciples when they are fishing (John 21:1–19). They have caught no fish and Jesus, after pointing this out to them, suggests they cast their nets on the other side of the boat. They haul in an enormous catch. Jesus' appearance to the disciples this time might seem to be all about abundance, but Peter and Jesus have unfinished business, a matter of sin. It is after they have eaten a breakfast of bread and fish that Jesus has prepared for them that Jesus and Peter have the conversation that we heard as our second reading. The location is important. Jesus returns to the scene of Peter's denial, the fire of coals, and his conversation with Peter is patterned on the conversation with the servant girl. Jesus does not spare himself the pain of the memory of Peter's sin—it is almost as if the nails are hammered in again—in fact, he deliberately goes there. Jesus does not spare Peter the pain of that memory either. Surprising, perhaps, that he did not have a cockerel waiting in the wings. Only Peter did not need a reminder of Jesus' deep understanding of human nature this time.

Peter just needed the guts to sit still and bear the questions. The three questions. "Do you love me?" Jesus asked Peter. "You know that I love you," Peter replied. "Feed my sheep." Jesus said.

It's an interesting question, this "Do you love me?" If Jesus had whispered it to Peter as he denied him by the fire of coals, the answer would have been the same. "You know that I love you, but I'm not brave enough. . . . I don't know him." "You know that I love you . . . but it's not enough to face what you are facing." "Lord, you know that I love you, but . . . "

Peter is no different; he is still the same flawed man, the man who stepped out across the water and then panicked, the one who insisted that Jesus not wash his feet, failing completely to understand what Jesus was on about, the one who promised to follow him wherever he went and then denied him. Peter is still Peter. The one who loves Jesus, who has always loved Jesus.

What matters is that he stays and hears the questions. "This is what you did. You denied me three times at the time when I needed you most. Let us remember what you did. Let us both remember the pain of what you did. And then you can know yourself forgiven. Each question washes away your sin. You are forgiven." Only in the place of sin can we know ourselves forgiven.

And then . . . "Feed my sheep," Jesus says. It is an extraordinary thing that Jesus is not only forgiving Peter but telling him he is to care for Jesus' people. He is fit for something. Flawed, but fit, fitted through forgiveness.

I will, I will, I myself will, says God. I will search for my sheep and seek them out and seek them out again, even if I have to die in the attempt, and break through the bonds of death, and seek out the lost on the other side.

Jesus is no different now. Sitting by the fires of coals where our sins were committed, wondering if we will ever find the courage to meet him there. We love him, in our motley sort of way; it's not that we don't, but he'll ask us the question anyway. Do you love me? We do but our love wasn't strong enough to stop our denials when the fear got the better of us, or the pride or the vanity, whatever it was.

His forgiveness changes everything, though. We don't believe in it until we experience it. We don't believe he could forgive us; we certainly wouldn't forgive ourselves. We give up on ourselves, but he is waiting, just longing for us to hear his questions, bear the pain of them, so that he might set us free.

His forgiveness changes everything. It restored Peter. It will restore us. "Do you love me?" searching through heaven and earth to search us out. "Do you love me?" "Yes Lord, you know that I love you." "Feed my sheep then. Search for my sheep and seek them out and seek them out again. Even if you have to die in the attempt, feed my sheep."

CHAPTER 17

Pondering Joy and Pain—Mary

The film *Shadowlands* tells the story of C. S. Lewis and the woman, Joy, he meets later in his life, falls in love with, and marries. Joy is terminally ill, and a scene towards the end of the film shows C. S. Lewis, whom Joy calls Jack, and Joy travelling to visit one of his favourite places, the Golden Valley in Herefordshire, close to Wales. Joy speaks with Jack about the situation in which they find themselves. Jack doesn't want the conversation, doesn't want to speak about the reality that Joy will die, that their happiness will not last. She needs him to hear her say one thing, as she believes that he can only be truly with her when she dies if he understands this one thing. She needs him to know that the pain when she dies is part of the happiness they know now.

The pain then is part of the happiness now. That's the deal. But it's not just that. It's not just that the pain that Joy and Jack will know in the future, when she is dying, and when she dies, is in some essential way woven together with the happiness they know as they drive through the countryside and eventually find the valley he so longed to show her. It's not just that. It's that she believes that knowing the interwovenness of the happiness and the pain is better than just managing. That knowing this is somehow being the best they can be.

The pain then is part of the happiness now.

I think Mary knew this.

I think Mary, whose life as mother of Jesus we are thinking about, knew this. I think every story that is told about her, every painting, every icon drawn and gazed upon, hints that she knew this. Mary knew the truth that the deepest way of living life is to know and to live out of the fact that when you love someone pain and joy are interwoven. Reflecting upon her life, though we really know little of it, and for some, praying in her company, can help us to know this truth too.

Mary knew about living the truth bravely and honestly. We see this firstly in the story of the Annunciation. Mary is a young woman whose betrothal to the good man Joseph means that her life is set out for her. Gabriel interrupts her young life. He brings greetings from God and he tells her that she is not to be afraid, for she has found favour with God. Then Gabriel tells Mary that she will conceive in her womb and bear a son, whom she will name Jesus. Mary embraces this meeting with her whole heart, her whole being. She embraces the fear she experiences when this God messenger interrupts her life; we know that as Gabriel tells her not to be afraid. She embraces his request. She ponders what is being asked of her. This word, ponder, means gives weight to. Mary treats as weighty, worthy of deep thought, her encounters with angels and what they tell her about her son. Nine months later, when Jesus is born and the shepherds visit Joseph and Mary and their baby in the stable and tell them about that baby, again Mary gives weight to the shepherds' words. Luke writes that Mary treasures all that the shepherds said and ponders those words too in her heart.

In that first scene in which we meet Mary, when Gabriel announces that she will bear a son, Mary wrestles with Gabriel. Mary is not passive. "How can this be?" she asks the angel. How can it be that she can be with child when she is a virgin? She wants to understand what God is doing, how God will bring this blessing upon her. And then Gabriel explains, "The Holy Spirit will come upon you, and the power of the Most High will overshadow you.... For nothing will be impossible with God". Mary struggles with fear and questions, ponders, and only when Gabriel makes it clear that his message is about God at work does she then give her assent. Mary bravely, honestly, lives the truth (Luke 1:26–38).

Mary then journeys to visit her cousin Elizabeth. Elizabeth names her blessed, the Mother of the Lord. Mary understands what is happening to her, understands this blessing. Each encounter she is given helps her understand the life as Jesus' mother to which God is calling her. But she understands because she listens, she wonders, she embraces what she is bring told. And then the joy overflows in her. Only after she has so honestly struggled with fear and doubt and disbelief at what the angel has told her, only after she has heard the witness of Elizabeth and Elizabeth's child, does the joy of being the Mother of the Lord overflow in her (Luke 1:39-45).

And that joy overflows in song—the *Magnificat* that we sing at Evensong each Sunday night—the Song of Mary in which she rejoices in God and what God is doing in her, a lowly woman. And she expresses her deep understanding of God's ways. God intends peace for our earth and salvation for all, particularly those on the margins. Mary's song, infused with the radical theology of the Old Testament, leaves us in no doubt that God's embrace is wide and reverses the values of our world. God, in choosing Mary, who is lowliness herself, will bring down the powerful from their thrones, and lift up the lowly, will fill the hungry with good things and send the rich away empty (Luke 1:52-4).

Mary knows the truth that the deepest way of living life is to know and to live out of the fact that, when you love someone, pain and joy are interwoven.

It is not long after her son is born that the shadow of the pain of loving crosses her path. Mary and Joseph encounter the devout old man Simeon when they take Jesus for the rite of purification in the temple. Simeon speaks the words that we sing at Evensong as the *Nunc Dimittis* naming Jesus as the Saviour of the whole world. Then Simeon blesses them and says to Mary, "This child is destined for the falling and the rising of many in Israel, and to be a sign that will be opposed so that the inner thoughts of many will be revealed—and a sword will pierce your own soul too" (Luke 2:34-5). . . . "a sword will pierce your own soul too". And the shadow of the pain of loving passes over them.

And Mary finds herself thirty years or so later at the foot of a cross on which her adult son is dying.

The pain then is part of the happiness now. That is the deal. The deal for Joy and C. S. Lewis as they faced Joy's dying. The deal for Mary, Mother of our Lord, a young woman who knew about living the truth, who bravely, honestly, lived the truth. The truth is that when you love someone joy and pain are woven together, a joy and pain that finds redemption in Mary's Son, Jesus, living and dying and rising to new life.

CHAPTER 18

Nurturing the Soul—Music Sunday

The word "*fieri*", the name of our choir in residence this week, means "become". This is a word, an idea, with no small theological meaning. That we as human beings, that our visitors as a group of singers, that our planet, that creation even, are in a place of *becoming* is a truth given by God who created us. We are made but we are not static. We are not yet complete. God has created us in love, but God's work is not yet done. We are in a place of becoming. The word "*fieri*" describes us too.

Before we ponder the place of music in these things, on this our Music Sunday, before we ponder how music nurtures our "becoming" in God, we need to spend a little time with what is indeed a most challenging Gospel reading (Matthew 15:21–8). We might find that, in this reading, not only are the characters who encounter Jesus undergoing a change—embracing their "becoming" if you like—but that this is true of Jesus too. We will reflect on what it might mean that Jesus allows himself to embrace the process that this reading seems to strongly imply he undergoes.

Jesus has just been challenged by the religious leaders, the Pharisees and the scribes, about his disciples' failure to observe the religious laws about washing their hands before they eat. In a long exchange, Jesus, with the leaders and then with the crowd that has gathered around, explores what it is that truly renders a person unclean. The religious leaders are offended by Jesus' challenge to them. Jesus then goes into Gentile territory, into the district of Tyre and Sidon, presumably to have a break from such challenging encounters. But a Canaanite woman from the region will not let him rest. She cries out to him, three times, begging him to heal her daughter who is possessed by a demon. *She* is about to challenge *him*, this time, about who is clean, about who belongs. We find that, unlike the religious leaders in the previous scene, the woman is far from offended by Jesus' response to her. She perseveres until he gives her that for which she asks.

"Have mercy on me, Lord, Son of David," the woman cries, at first, identifying Jesus as a leader in the Jewish faith, but he does not answer her at all. Jesus' disciples come and urge him to send her away. Jesus, though, does speak to her: "I was sent only to the lost sheep of the house of Israel." He is saying that she does not belong to the group to whom he has come to bring life. Abandoning the Jewish title, "Son of David," the woman comes and kneels before Jesus, saying, simply, "Lord, help me". She brings only her vulnerability, her longing for the daughter she loves to be healed. Jesus answers, "It is not fair to take the children's food and throw it to the dogs". We need to understand what he is saying here. He is not insulting the woman as it might first appear. In that culture, non-Jewish people were referred to as dogs. Jesus is saying that, because the woman is not a Jew, he is not there to heal her daughter. Speaking a third time, the woman says, "Yes, Lord, yet even the dogs eat the crumbs that fall from their masters' table". The woman uses Jesus' own image to challenge him, to teach him.

We know Jesus is the consummate teacher, one who uses parables involving images from ordinary life to give those around him insight into the ways of God. This woman, this outsider, plays him at his own game. She subverts his image. She is clearly broadening the scope of Jesus' healing power, engaging with the image Jesus has employed and using it to challenge him. The Canaanite woman sees a breadth to Jesus' capacity to heal that it seems he does not yet see. *She* converts *him* and Jesus answers her, "Woman, great is your faith! Let it be done for you as you wish". And her daughter is healed instantly. Jesus' view of the woman is transformed. The one he had named a dog, an outsider, he now calls "Woman". Through this woman he has become a little more who he is, the one who brings healing to the world.

We might ponder this encounter a little more deeply, for it is puzzling. Is this a battle scene? Are Jesus and the woman fighting, a fight that the woman wins? We would surely struggle a little with this—for it seems incongruent with everything else we know about Jesus.

It is possible that the key characteristic of Jesus, the offering of vulnerability that we see on the cross—might give a lens on this story that will help. We remember that, in what is known as the Philippians Hymn, Paul writes that Jesus "emptied himself . . . humbled himself, becoming obedient to the point of death, even death on a cross" (Philippians 2:7-8). We might also remember that, in another healing story, when a woman with a haemorrhage which has plagued her for twelve years touches Jesus, he becomes aware that power has gone forth from him (Mark 5:30). In the exchange between Jesus and the Canaanite woman, again, Jesus loses power, Jesus is humbled. He engages with the woman, allowing her to overpower him with her faith and her insight into God's desire to heal. This is not about a fight that Jesus loses, so much as a humbling engagement that Jesus allows.

Through her faith, through the power of her love for her daughter, the woman in this story becomes the one who not only brings healing to that daughter, but is the one who helps Jesus become more deeply who he is. His engagement with this, though, is of the nature of his engagement in his whole life and particularly in his death—an engagement of humility. Jesus allows this engagement to take place; he allows his limited understanding of himself to be exposed by a foreign woman.

In the Gospel stories there are many accounts of Jesus' healing of one who is suffering. These stories have a pattern. In each healing story, Jesus acts in humility allowing the one who suffers to cry out, to reach out and, in the case of the Canaanite woman, to argue with him, in order that healing may take place. In every case Jesus allows the one who is healed or who asks for the healing of a loved one to find their faith, to *become a person of faith*, and through their becoming, to bring out healing from him, to enable him to become the one who heals. Jesus acts in humility, as the one who asks for healing acts in faith. Both are blessed, both become more deeply who God has made them to be.

This engagement through humility has resonances with the way we engage with music. This morning we are blessed by music, by the beautiful Mass setting by Christopher Tye into which our Eucharist is woven; last night, in the concert entitled "Out of the Shadows", we were blessed by music that explored the concept of transgression—legal, moral and spiritual—and humanity's journey towards redemption. When we allow ourselves to be touched by music, we approach it with humility, with vulnerability; we allow it to reach us, possibly even to transform us;

we allow music to open our eyes to the beauty and the struggle of life, to the possibility of God and love and redemption. Our encounter with music is not unlike Jesus' encounter with those who come to him for healing, not unlike their encounter with him.

Fieri, becoming.

The presence of the Fieri Consort with us this week and particularly this morning, reminds us of the profound significance of music in the life of this cathedral, music that nurtures our growth, our becoming as children of God. We offer our heartfelt thanks to Hannah, Helen and Lucy, Ben, David, Josh and Tom, The Fieri Consort, who have come into our midst to sing and to teach, to inspire and to share friendship. We are deeply grateful to our Music Foundation for sponsoring the Fieri Consort's visit; we are grateful to the Music Foundation for supporting the fundraising for the restoration of our cathedral organ. The courage we have shown in embarking on this project is a courage in which we are claiming our identity as a sacred place dedicated to the performance of and education in fine music. This cathedral is indeed a place where prayer is nurtured in beautiful music and fine liturgy, where prayer is nurtured in the midst of people who have gathered to ponder what it is to be given the gift of life, to know the struggles and blessings of life, and to glimpse the truth that the God who made us continues to bless us as we become the children God made us to be.

PART 5

Coming Home—In the Gospel of Luke

CHAPTER 19

Anointing by the Spirit

Luke's Gospel opens with the accounts of two homecomings. Two couples find themselves expecting children. The one, a couple ancient in years, has always longed for a child—and God hears finally their longing—and grants them their hearts' desire. Zechariah and Elizabeth will give birth to John the Baptist, the one who will herald Christ's coming and who will baptize him as his ministry commences.

The other couple is only betrothed to be married. The angel Gabriel, God's messenger, appears to Mary and asks her to bear God's son. Will she allow him a home on this earth, that he might show us the way to be home in God? That is her calling. That is the calling of her son. She is courage itself and assents to allowing him a home in her and with her, a home that will put her at great risk and cause her great pain. The scholar Brendan Byrne's book *The Hospitality of God* greatly influenced me in the writing of this sermon series. He wrote of Mary, "She is the first in a long line of characters in this Gospel who give hospitality to Jesus only to find themselves drawn into the hospitality of God".[22]

This Jesus is utterly at home in his Father, God. All his earthly life is lived out of his closeness to God. All his encounters with human beings are nurtured there. And his journey to Jerusalem, a journey that ends in death, is walked in God. And Jesus lives this life and dies this death that we and all creation too might find our home in God.

In this sermon series, we will explore this theme of "Coming Home" in St Luke's Gospel. Christ is at home in God. God's longing is that we might also know our home to be in God. In five sermons we will look at different aspects of Jesus' ministry—his receiving of the Spirit; his healing; his love of meals with, particularly, those whom society shuns; his teaching through those strange stories, the parables; and his guidance on the way to live in God. The two other great events in the Gospel, Christ's death and his resurrection, and Luke's treatment of those events, we will ponder at the proper time—on Good Friday and on Easter night.

Two homecomings on earth—the births of John and Jesus. Each are heralded with song—the *Benedictus* and the *Magnificat* that we hear sung each Sunday night in this cathedral at Evensong. When Zechariah sings the *Benedictus*, he says the words, "By the tender mercy of our God, the dawn from on high will break upon us, to give light to those who sit in darkness and in the shadow of death, to guide our feet into the way of peace" (Luke 1:78–9). This is what Jesus is about—salvation. God intends peace for our earth and salvation for all, particularly those on the margins. Mary's song, infused with the radical theology of the Old Testament, leaves us in no doubt that God's embrace is wide and reverses the values of our world. God, in choosing Mary, who is lowliness herself, will bring down the powerful from their thrones, and lift up the lowly, will fill the hungry with good things and send the rich away empty (Luke 1:52–4). As we explore Jesus' ministry, we will find his mother's words fulfilled.

Here we will ponder Jesus as one infused by the Spirit, one who is utterly at home in God. Jesus enters Luke's Gospel scene as an adult when his cousin is baptizing the crowds by the River Jordan. Jesus too is baptized and while he is at prayer, God's voice is heard. Jesus is always praying. Luke portrays Jesus at prayer before so many significant events in the Gospel.

After Jesus is baptized, " . . . and is praying, the heavens opened, and the Holy Spirit descended upon him in bodily form like a dove. And a voice came from heaven, 'You are my Son, the Beloved; with you I am well pleased'" (Luke 3:21–2). Jesus' identity is clear. He is God's Son, God's Beloved.

Jesus, though, quickly embraces his home on earth: "Jesus, full of the Holy Spirit, returned from the Jordan and was led by the Spirit in the wilderness, where for forty days he was tempted by the devil" (Luke 4:1–2).

He enters into the heart of human life—temptation and suffering and struggle. As Brendan Byrne writes, "Precisely *as* God's Son, obedient to the pattern of divine love and grace that drives him, he will enter fully into the human lot of suffering and death.... Son of Adam as well as Son of God, he will enter into the pain and evil of the world to work the inner transformation that alone will render it hospitable to God".[23]

Jesus opens his ministry in his hometown, at the synagogue in Nazareth, on the Sabbath day. A true Jewish teacher, he reads from the scroll of the prophet Isaiah:

> "The Spirit of the Lord is upon me,
> because he has anointed me
> to bring good news to the poor.
> He has sent me to proclaim release to the captives
> and recovery of sight to the blind,
> to let the oppressed go free,
> to proclaim the year of the Lord's favour."
>
> *Luke 4:18–19*

Luke's is a spirit-filled Gospel. At the Annunciation, Mary is told by Gabriel that "the Holy Spirit will come upon you and the power of the Most High will overshadow you" (Luke 1:35). The Spirit sent Christ, and the Spirit anointed Christ for his adult ministry. The power at work in him is the power of God's Spirit. But the one anointed by God's Spirit is not always made welcome.

We are warned of this right at the beginning of Jesus' ministry in Nazareth: "The eyes of all in the synagogue were fixed on him. Then he began to say to them, 'Today this scripture has been fulfilled in your hearing'. All spoke well of him and were amazed at the gracious words that came from his mouth. They said, 'Is not this Joseph's son?' ... And he said, 'Truly I tell you, no prophet is accepted in the prophet's home town'" (Luke 4:20–4).

And the rejection begins.

All through the opening scenes of Luke's Gospel, and particularly in this scene in the synagogue in Nazareth, Jesus is anointed by the Spirit in the way of the prophets of old. His earthly life will bear much in common with the lives of the Jewish prophets—lives of poverty, lives without a settled home, lives of rejection, and lives of prayer.

One Jesuit, Walter Burghardt, wrote of prayer as taking "a long loving look at the real".[24] Is that what Jesus did, up on his mountains, held in the Spirit, is that what he did? Did he take a long loving look at the real, at what was about him? Did he look at the river and the sea and the plains? At the synagogues where his Father's words were read and pondered and yet, where those who called themselves religious so often struggled to know God at all? Did he take a long loving look at those who were hungry and those who were possessed by the voices that drowned out his Father's voice, calling them "Beloved"? Was his loving gaze offered to those whose lives were broken by illness, illness that had them shunned by those who might have been community for them? Later we'll keep watch with him alongside those who were sick and those who were possessed. We'll see how he brings them home.

It's Lent now. That long Sabbath time.

The time to remember that we are dust and to dust we shall return. Dust made by God. The time to sit with the truth that we are created by God, in love, from the dust. The time to make our fast and give our alms. The time for stillness and quiet thought. The time for repentance. The time for gratitude.

It is the time for us to sit still. Shall we keep him company on his mountain at prayer? Knowing that however faint that voice might be, somewhere God is calling us, and all creation, "Beloved" too? Shall we take a long loving look at the real? Believing or struggling to believe that he is with us? That the Spirit that bathed his prayer might nurture our own? Shall we sit with him, listening to his voice, that quiet and yet relentless voice? That voice that will seek us out wherever we are and however far from God we think we might be, that voice of forgiveness, that voice of love, calling us home.

CHAPTER 20

Healing as Homecoming

There are few whom Jesus meets, in Luke's Gospel, who are *farther from home* than the man possessed by demons in the country of Gerasenes. In Luke 8, Jesus, who has just calmed a storm on the lake, finds himself in the presence of another storm. He meets a demon-possessed man over on the *other* side of the lake, in Gentile territory. For a long time, the man has worn no clothes, and he does not live in a house but in the tombs. The man is kept under guard and bound with chains and shackles, but he repeatedly breaks the bonds and is driven by the demons into the wilds (Luke 8:27,29). All the signs point to the fact that this possessed man is an *outsider* in every way—he is out of his mind, living outside a home, and he is far away from Jewish territory.

In this, our second in this sermon series exploring Jesus as the one sent by God to bring us home, we will explore the idea of *healing as homecoming*. In our first sermon we encountered Jesus as one infused by the Spirit, one who is utterly at home in God. We saw that Luke portrays Jesus at prayer before so many significant events in the Gospel, and we pondered the idea that prayer might be thought of as taking "a long, loving look at the real". Jesus does this with whomever he meets, even a man from whom most would run away—someone possessed by demons. We might spend a moment thinking about those demons. Demons speak against the voice of God. God, we remember from last week, calls Jesus, and all that God has made, "Beloved". The demon voices, the voices of negativity, attempt to drown out God's voice, tell us it cannot be that we are "Beloved", tell us we cannot be the person God has called us to be. It is unusual that one would be so affected that they would live the life of the naked deranged man in the Gerasenes, but we are all affected by voices that challenge God's loving voice.

When Jesus steps out of the boat, the man possessed by demons meets him. When the man approaches Jesus, Jesus commands the unclean spirit to come out of him, and he falls down before him and shouts at the top of his voice, "What have you to do with me, Jesus, Son of the Most High God? I beg you, do not torment me". Jesus then asks him, "What is your name?" He says, "Legion"; for many demons had entered him. They beg him not to order them to go back into the abyss, back where they came from (Luke 8:27,28,30).

The demons know who Jesus is. Because Jesus stays around. Jesus goes very close to this man; he takes a long loving look at him, if you like, and does not run away. Sometimes loving is about not running away. Sometimes care of those who are ill or disturbed involves staying put.

Simone Weil wrote:

> Those who are unhappy have no need for anything in this world but people capable of giving them their attention. The capacity to give one's attention to a sufferer is a rare and difficult thing; it is almost a miracle; it is a miracle.[25]

We cannot know if Jesus is frightened by this possessed man or not, but whatever he feels, Jesus *is* that miracle; he stays and engages with him. Jesus engages with the demons and casts them out. And when people come out to see what has happened, they find the man from whom the demons have gone sitting at the feet of Jesus, clothed and in his right mind. We might think he has found his home at Jesus' side, but Jesus has other ideas about that. When the healed man asks to stay with Jesus, Jesus sends him away, saying, "Return to your home, and declare how much God has done for you" (Luke 8:38–9). Homecoming is about being healed and sharing the good news of God's healing. And that healing comes from Jesus' determined presence, a presence that is offered to all.

Illness often excludes. Those who are ill cannot thrive in the life of their community. The woman who had been suffering from haemorrhages for twelve years who came up behind Jesus and touched the fringe of his clothes would have been considered unclean in her community. She was unclean, and any whom she touched, including Jesus, would have been made unclean by that touch. He is not concerned about that, though.

He feels the power go out of him and knows that a woman has been healed but there is more to this healing than the stopping of the woman's haemorrhage. Jesus wants her to know the role she has played in her being made well (Luke 8:43–6).

Most healing stories involve a cry, a cry of faith, or a cry of the struggle for faith. Healing stories are exodus stories, really. They involve God freeing a person or a people who are enslaved in some way by illness, an illness that traps them away from home. God engaged with the people of Israel in slavery in Egypt, when God heard them cry out, and God set his people free. When Jesus heals, he heals in response to a cry of the one who is sick or one who knows them.

The story of the healing of the woman with the haemorrhages is enfolded in another healing story, the story of the healing of Jairus' daughter. Jairus cried out to Jesus on behalf of his dying daughter, begging him to come to his house to heal her (Luke 8:41–2). The haemorrhaging woman "cries out" to Jesus by touching the fringe of his clothes. Jesus' healings seem to involve the meeting of the faith of the one who is ill, or one who cares for them, with his compassion, with his long loving look at them. Jesus says to the woman who has been suffering with the haemorrhages, "Daughter, your faith has made you well; go in peace". Immediately after he has sent the healed woman home, Jesus is met with the news that Jairus' daughter has died. Luke has interwoven these two healing stories to highlight the importance of faith in healing. "Do not fear. Only believe, and she will be saved", Jesus says to the girl's distraught father. He goes to Jairus' house, commands his daughter to "get up" and tells her parents to give her something to eat. A family meal is about to take place. Jairus' home has been restored (Luke 8:48–50,54–5).

Jesus' courageous and compassionate presence casts out demons and heals disease, especially in the presence of the faith expressed in him by those who are ill or those who love them. Jesus' "long loving look" at the struggle of those he encounters brings them home.

Only it doesn't always seem to. When we live with an illness that it seems will not go away, or when we watch a loved one die from an illness that was not healed, or when we know someone or find ourselves with struggles, physical or emotional, that just seem to be part of who we are, we might wonder what all these stories about Jesus healing might mean. I wonder if, at times like this, we might remember that man in the Gerasenes, because struggling, or watching another we love struggle, with a disease can leave us some days feeling a little like that man who was naked and homeless and overwhelmed. And we might imagine Jesus getting out of a boat on the other side of a lake, far away from home and sitting with us. Just sitting with us. We might imagine that. That however far from home we experience ourselves to be, or one we love to be, he will come and sit with us and will not leave us alone.

It's our cry that matters. Our expression of the truth. The cry of the demons in the possessed man. Or the cry of the woman as she touches Jesus' clothes. Or the cry of Jairus for his daughter. It's telling God the truth of our life, and the lives of those we love, that matters. And he may restore us as we hope to be restored. The woman who bled for most of her adult life may be healed. The girl may rise up to eat a meal with her family. The man may find his place by Jesus, clothed and in his right mind. But we know well that may not be granted. And if it's not, then pouring out our truth to God is what matters. And he'll be there. Jesus won't leave us alone. And we might find that sitting with him, speaking the truth of our longing for healing will, strangely, be home.

CHAPTER 21

Sharing in God's Embrace

Jesus loved sinners. Jesus loves sinners. A few verses before our first reading, from Luke 7, Jesus says, "The Son of Man has come eating and drinking, and you say, 'Look, a glutton and a drunkard, a friend of tax collectors and sinners!'" (Luke 7:34).

Jesus seems greatly to enjoy the company of tax collectors and sinners, and this was best expressed in his eating meals with them. Luke's Gospel contains numerous accounts of Jesus feeding and being fed, of Jesus hosting and being invited to meals, with the attendant disapproving comment we have come to expect from the religious leaders watching from nearby.

In this, the third sermon in our series exploring Jesus as the one sent by God to bring us home, we will explore the idea of Jesus' meals as images of home, images of God's embrace. In recent weeks, we have seen Jesus as one infused by the Spirit, one who is utterly at home in God. We saw his mother Mary, overshadowed by the Holy Spirit, welcoming the son sent by God to turn the ways of the world upside down. Mary's song, the *Magnificat*, leaves us in no doubt that God's embrace is wide and reverses the values of our world. God, among other things, will fill the hungry with good things and send the rich away empty (Luke 1:52-4).

And before we get all sentimental about this, it is worth our imagining for a moment the sort of people with whom Jesus spent his time, the sort of people in whose company he, in fact, delighted. The word for sin, in Greek, "*hamartia*", literally means "missing the mark". In the Jewish culture, sinners were those who did not follow the Jewish law, the Torah. They were outsiders. Tax collectors were greatly disliked. Often greedy and dishonest, they collected indirect taxes such as those placed on the transportation of goods. And Jewish wisdom held that friendship should only be encouraged with those of the *same kind*. One wisdom writing states "Be on your guard and very careful, for you are walking about with your own downfall ... What does a wolf have in common with a lamb? No more has a sinner with the devout" (Sirach 13:13–17). Eating with sinners was just not done.

Imagine Jesus sitting down to a meal with a politician you utterly distrust, with someone who has committed a violent crime, with a businessman whose ethics you seriously doubt. Jesus is not just "tolerating" the strange company he keeps; he is positively revelling in it. Only when we can imagine ourselves being shocked by the meals in which he seems to delight can the power of these stories affect us, move us, convert us. Who would we least like to spend an evening with? That's the company Jesus keeps. And worse than that; that's the company Jesus treasures. It's not that he approves of sin, far from it. But he will not allow the fact that a person is repugnant to society, for whatever reason, to stop him embracing them.

And on occasion they respond with an embrace.

> One of the Pharisees asked Jesus to eat with him, and he went into the Pharisee's house and took his place at the table. And a woman in the city, who was a sinner, having learned that he was eating in the Pharisee's house, brought an alabaster jar of ointment. She stood behind him at his feet, weeping, and began to bathe his feet with her tears and to dry them with her hair. Then she continued kissing his feet and anointing them with the ointment. Now when the Pharisee who had invited him saw it, he said to himself, "If this man were a prophet, he would have known who and what kind of woman this is who is touching him—that she is a sinner."
>
> *Luke 7:36–9*

Jesus knew. And he tells a parable that affirms that the woman, who has—embarrassingly, really—lavished such a display of affection for Jesus, is a sinner. But the parable makes the point that this woman knows she is welcome in Jesus' presence, that she has much to be grateful for. Jesus is almost ferocious is his comparison of the woman's hospitality to him with Simon the Pharisee's lack of hospitality. She bathed Jesus' feet, kissed them and anointed them with oil. Simon offered no such welcome. Great love is expressed by those who are forgiven much. "Your sins are forgiven", Jesus says to the woman. As if she doesn't know. "Your faith has saved you. Go in peace" (Luke 7:48,50). Those gathered at the table with Jesus can only wonder who it is that can forgive sins in this way. Who's the sinner now? Who is the one failing to allow God to be God?

Meals have special significance in Jewish culture. One scholar put it this way:

> In the east, even today, to invite a person to a meal was an honor. It was an offer of peace, truth, brotherhood, and forgiveness. In short, sharing a table meant sharing life. In Judaism in particular, table fellowship means fellowship before God.... [Jesus' meals] are an expression of the mission and message of Jesus ... anticipatory celebrations of the feast at the end time.... The inclusion of sinners in the company of salvation, achieved in table fellowship, is the most meaningful expression of the message of the redeeming love of God.[26]

Sharing a table means sharing life.

In some of Luke's stories Jesus invites himself to a meal:

> [Jesus] entered Jericho and was passing through it. A man was there named Zacchaeus; he was a chief tax-collector and was rich. He was trying to see who Jesus was, but on account of the crowd he could not, because he was short in stature. So he ran ahead and climbed a sycamore tree to see him, because he was going to pass that way. When Jesus came to the place, he looked up and said to him, "Zacchaeus, hurry and come down; for I must stay at your house today." So he hurried down and was happy to welcome him. All who saw it began to grumble and said, "He has gone to be the guest of one who is a sinner."
>
> *Luke 19:1–7*

Zacchaeus is excluded in two ways. He is too short to see Jesus above the crowd, and he is yet another of the hated tax collectors. Not unlike the woman who pours expensive ointment on Jesus' feet, not unlike the woman with the haemorrhage who pushed through the crowd to touch Jesus' garment, Zacchaeus goes to extravagant lengths to reach Jesus. Jesus affirms the faith of both these women, and he is affirming of Zacchaeus as well. He invites himself to Zacchaeus' home. Jesus says that he "must" stay at Zacchaeus' home, an indication that this is God's desire, God's purpose. Zacchaeus hurries down and is happy to welcome Jesus. The crowd grumble.

Zacchaeus immediately announces his intention of changing his ways—he will give half his possessions to the poor, and if he has defrauded anyone of anything, he will repay them four times. In a previous sermon, we saw Jesus open his ministry in his hometown, at the synagogue in Nazareth, on the Sabbath day with a quotation from the prophet Isaiah. "Today," he said, "this scripture has been fulfilled in your hearing." Jesus responds to Zacchaeus with words reminiscent of this great "today" spoken in Nazareth, "Today salvation has come to this house," he says (Luke 19:9). Salvation for Luke is shown here when Jesus seeks out an excluded and sinful man, a man who in Jesus' presence finds there the strength to repent of his sin. In this story, we see that as Zacchaeus welcomes Jesus into his home, he finds himself welcomed into the home of God.

As in the story of the meal at Simon the Pharisee's house, we find ourselves wondering who the sinner is now. Who knows themselves at home in Jesus' presence now as he enjoys a meal under Zacchaeus' hospitality? The resentful and grumbling crowd seem to be the ones who are far from home.

Sharing a table means sharing life.

And we have seen that, in Luke's Gospel, Jesus shares his table with many whom society would shun, many of whom we might think God would disapprove. God welcomes those we struggle to welcome; God, in fact, delights in their company. There is another thing, another side to this strange welcoming way of God that we might ponder. And that is that God welcomes and delights in the part of *us* with which we struggle. Hidden in us, *well* hidden in us, usually, is something we have done wrong, or a way of being of which we are ashamed.. Hidden in us is some aspect of us—perhaps it is pride or greed or resentment—that we assume God would reject, we assume God would not want to share a table with, if you like. But these stories from Luke's Gospel give us a hint of a perhaps shocking truth. These stories might lead us to wonder if it is, in fact, precisely those parts of us of which we are most ashamed that God longs to embrace; it is those ways of being that we wish we didn't have that God longs to gather home; it is the very part of us that we would most wish to hide to which God says, "I must stay at your house today".

CHAPTER 22

Do Anything to Get Home

> Now all the tax-collectors and sinners were coming near to listen to him. And the Pharisees and the scribes were grumbling and saying, "This fellow welcomes sinners and eats with them."
>
> Luke 15:1–2

In our last sermon, as we continued our exploration of Jesus as the one sent by God to bring us home, we explored the idea of Jesus' meals as images of home, images of God's embrace. We saw Jesus, the one who knows himself to be utterly at home in God, eating with tax collectors and sinners, with those whom society shunned. We discussed the meaning of meals in Jewish culture; we explored the ideas of scholars; we wondered about the part we played in making some feel outcast; and we even pondered the idea that some aspects of ourselves are outcast too.

Jesus did none of this. In response to the religious leaders' protestations at the company he kept, Jesus told stories. In Luke 15 we see Jesus respond to the grumbling Pharisees and scribes, by telling three parables, the Parable of the Lost Coin, the Parable of the Lost Sheep and the Parable of the Prodigal Son, or, as it is sometimes known, "the parable of the two sons".

Jesus drives the point home, in these three stories, that God is almost ridiculous in the efforts God will put in to search out those who are lost. A shepherd has a hundred sheep and loses one. "Which one of you, [Jesus asks], having a hundred sheep and losing one of them, does not leave the ninety-nine in the wilderness and go after the one that is lost until he finds it?" (Luke 15:4). Which of us, indeed? The question is telling. For many of us would find ourselves wondering if we would, in fact, go after that lost sheep. These parables are told not only to give us insight into the nature of this ever-searching God; they are told to shine a light onto the nature of human beings, the ones who grumble when the lost are embraced, the ones who probably would not engage in the relentless search.

"What woman having ten silver coins, if she loses one of them, does not light a lamp, sweep the house, and search carefully until she finds it?" (Luke 15:8). Again Jesus asks a probing question. This is what God is like; but what are you like? The woman's response is critical and matches that of the shepherd, not grudging relief, but delight, joy, the gathering of friends and neighbours to celebrate. Grumbling, rejoicing—these two responses are placed in sharp relief in these three parables, not least in the third, the parable of the two sons. A son takes his father's inheritance, and then, on this son's return, his father rejoices, and extravagantly so. His brother's response matches that of the religious leaders; he is angry and refuses to join in the celebrations. His father speaks with him, and that is where the stories end. Jesus leaves us to ponder the possibilities of joy and resentment as responses to our witness of God's embrace of those of whom we might disapprove.

We need to be careful, though, about assuming that Jesus' parables are easy to interpret. Many of them are baffling. I was most helped in pondering the parables by a lecturer who told us to find what it was in a parable that we didn't get. What most irritates us? Sit with what keeps you awake at night. Is it Jesus' pointed question about whether we would search out the lost? Is it the time wasted by the shepherd looking for the hundredth sheep? Is it the utter lack of pride in the father who races to greet his ungrateful son?

We don't have to look hard to find what baffles us in the parable of the dishonest manager from Luke 16. It is staggering. What can Jesus possibly mean by a story that concludes like this?

> [The] master commended the dishonest manager because he had acted shrewdly; for the children of this age are more shrewd in dealing with their own generation than are the children of light. And I tell you, make friends for yourselves by means of dishonest

wealth so that when it is gone, they may welcome you into the eternal homes.

Luke 16:8-9

When I had to reflect on this parable in a Friday morning service a few months ago, I ran in desperation to the commentaries for assistance. How could one make sense of a parable that seemed to encourage dishonesty? The scholar John Shea made a fascinating point. He compared the parable of the dishonest manager with the one immediately preceding it, the Parable of the Prodigal Son. Although we may struggle with the generosity of the father in this parable, or with the behaviour of either of the sons, we have a certain comfort that this story gives real insight into the nature of God and human beings. John Shea shows that these two parables have the same structure.[27] It works like this. The prodigal son and the dishonest manager are both given property, and they *squander the property* (Luke 15:13; 16:1). The phrase is the same. After a little while, the prodigal son *came to himself* (Luke 15:17), and after the manager is told that he will be dismissed, he *said to himself* (Luke 16:3). Both engage in reflection about their situation and take on some responsibility for it. They both develop a plan, not motivated by goodness but selfishness, a plan that will ensure their survival (Luke 15:18-19; 16:3-4). They both head for home. This is clear in the case of the prodigal son. Jesus explains it in the case of the dishonest manager as he praises his shrewdness. He says, "Make friends for yourselves by means of dishonest wealth so that when it is gone, they may welcome you into the eternal homes" (Luke 16:9).

The issue is getting home. Do anything to get home. Rush home and offer yourself as a hired hand for your father; make friends dishonestly, if that is what it takes. Whatever you can do to get yourself home is honoured by Jesus. The dynamic of these two parables is our dynamic, the human dynamic. We squander the property, the life, God gives us at times. And then, nurtured by God, we might "come to ourselves"; we might remember who we are—made by God, loved by God—and then we might realize that all that matters is getting home. If Jesus is saying anything in this strange parable, it might be this. Do anything to get home. For God will be there. God will be rushing to greet you; God will forgive before you even ask for forgiveness, *if* you even ask for forgiveness; and God will rejoice in your homecoming. Do anything to get home.

I have a confession to make. I found myself thinking, when I read this interpretation of this oh-so-difficult parable, that what seemed to matter was the desire for home in God, that, really, it needed a long run-up. That to be convinced by this interpretation I found myself wondering if one mightn't explore the *whole* of Luke's Gospel in the light of the theme of *home*. And so that is where this sermon series came from: the desire to explore surely one of the most difficult parables using the idea that God sent Christ to bring us home.

Jesus told stories. Rowan Williams, in his book *The Edge of Words*, in which he explores ways of speaking about God, put it this way: "We can speak, as Jesus does in the Gospel parables, through calling up a sequence of events, reactions and relations as a sort of complex metaphor. What is God like? 'There was a man who had two sons . . .' . . . God is represented by a whole narrative; to enter into the story and discover where you as a hearer fit and what role is possible for you to adopt imaginatively, is to become able to offer a representation that claims truthfulness . . . "[28]

Jesus told stories. What of us? Shall we see that, at times, we squander the life God gives us; shall we, like the prodigal son and the dishonest manager, come to ourselves, shall we do anything to get home? And then? When we get there? Shall we tell stories too? Shall we tell God our story? Shall we pour out the story of our life to him, that life, God-given and God-blessed, shall we pour out our story too? Shall we tell of our times of failure, tell of our guilt for sins committed? Shall we tell God of the times where we didn't let God be God? Shall we hear God's words of forgiveness? Is that what home's about? Shall we tell of our struggles, of those we love who are suffering? Shall we ask God to send healing upon them? Shall we pour out our gratitude to God for all the blessings given to us? One mystic, Meister Eckhart, remember, said that if we have said "thank you" we have said all the prayers, told all the stories, perhaps. Shall we thank God for the very blessing of life itself? Shall we tell God our stories?

Shall we do anything to get home and tell God our stories too?

CHAPTER 23

Heading Home

Coming home—in this series of sermons we have explored this theme in Luke's Gospel. We have watched Jesus particularly, this man born through the overshadowing of the Holy Spirit, born of his mother Mary. We have seen Mary assent to bearing God's son—to allowing him a home on this earth. We have seen this Jesus who is utterly at home in his Father, God, this God who named him "Beloved" at his baptism. All Jesus' earthly life is lived out of his closeness to God, all his encounters with human beings. And his journey to Jerusalem, a journey that ends in death, is walked in God. Jesus lives this life and dies this death that we and all creation too might find our home in God.

We have looked at different aspects of Jesus' ministry—his living a life of prayer, infused by the Spirit, prayer that we thought of as taking "a long loving look at the real". We have explored his healing, through the faith of those who cry out to him, and through his own compassion, his long loving look at those who are suffering. We have witnessed his love of meals with, particularly, those whom society shuns. We have wrestled with the parables he told. And we heard in the Parable of the Prodigal Son and the Parable of the Dishonest Manager, stories about two characters who, having squandered the life given to them, made extraordinary efforts to get home. And we heard Jesus say through these parables, "Do anything to get home".

Jesus is about salvation. God intends peace for our earth and salvation for all, particularly those on the margins. Mary's song that we hear sung each night at Evensong, leaves us in no doubt that God's embrace is wide and reverses the values of our world. God's project is to bring *all* creation home.

Through these sermons we have watched Jesus at work, but what of us? What is required of us as we journey, and encourage others on that journey, home?

> Just then a lawyer stood up to test Jesus. "Teacher," he said, "what must I do to inherit eternal life?" [Jesus] said to him, "What is written in the law? What do you read there?" He answered, "You shall love the Lord your God with all your heart, and with all your soul, and with all your strength, and with all your mind; and your neighbour as yourself." And he said to him, "You have given the right answer; do this, and you will live."
>
> *Luke 10:25-8*

Jesus met a lawyer who asked him what he must do to inherit eternal life. The lawyer in this story would have been one well versed in the Law of Moses. Jesus, as was often his way, answered the lawyer's question with another question. And so this teaching that combines two verses from the Jewish Law to love God and neighbour came from this lawyer's lips, not from the words of Jesus (Luke 10:25-8). We see the integrity Jesus gives to those who dare to engage with him—that the answers to such critical questions come from within themselves.

The lawyer goes on with the questions, though. "Who is my neighbour?" he asks, and Jesus responds with the Parable of the Good Samaritan (Luke 10:29-37). The lawyer seems to be asking for some sort of boundary to place around the idea of neighbour, for some restriction on those to whom Jesus might expect him to offer his neighbourly love. No restrictions here, though. Jesus tells a parable that seems to invite us to view this question from two perspectives. Firstly, we might ponder the experience of the beaten, half dead, man at the side of the road who watches two devout Jews pass by on the other side and then finds himself cared for by an outsider who views him with deep compassion. If we follow the questions, from the opening question "Who is my neighbour?" to Jesus' question at the end of the parable, "Which of these three, do you think, was a neighbour to the man who fell into the hands of the robbers?", we find that *we* are the wounded man and the Samaritan is *our* neighbour. And we find that the parable seems to be challenging us to love the utter stranger who cares for us in a time of need.

The second perspective in this parable is that of the passers-by. The priest and the Levite, strict followers of the Jewish law, would have been concerned that contact with this wounded man would have rendered them unclean. It is left to an outsider, a Samaritan, to show a different motivation. Jesus' audience would have been deeply shocked that it is a Samaritan used by Jesus to illustrate neighbourly behavior. Brendan Byrne states:

> At the end of the parable it is not a question of where and how far I should draw the limits of the notion "neighbour"—to see how far my obligations of "love" extend. It is a question of imitating the hospitality shown by the despised alien who broke through the barriers of ethnic and religious prejudice to minister to a fellow human being in need. The concept of "neighbour" shifts from being a tag that I may or may not apply to another, to being a quality or a vocation that I take upon myself and actively live out.[29]

The concept of neighbour is a *vocation*. And part of our way home is found in allowing this *vocation to neighbour* to infuse our lives.

And then we come to loving God. For loving God, living in the love of God, knowing ourselves enfolded in that love of God, somehow trying to return that love of God—is it possible that this is both the way home and that it *is home*?

Jesus is seen by the disciples praying in a "certain place", and they ask him to teach them how to pray. How do we love God? Is it in prayer? Pray, I think. Pray at all times and in all places. Tell God the truth. Know ourselves as children of God and live and breathe in that knowledge.

But who is this God? And will some sense of God help us as we try to pray?

Jesus knew God as Father and the first words of the prayer he gave us has us name God "Father". God, then, is like an utterly trustworthy parent. Jesus, when he spoke to the disciples about how to engage in this mysterious way of prayer, said to persevere; he told parables to encourage us to persevere, and he described God's longing to give the Holy Spirit to his children.

Rowan Williams describes God as an unconditional *witness*. He writes of "the unconditional witness to which/whom [we] seek to be open"[30] and of "the 'infinite resource' of God, the reality or presence that has no interest to pursue and no selfhood to defend".[31] All human beings, no matter how caring, have an interest to pursue and a selfhood to defend. Can we imagine being in the presence of God who, free from all self-interest, opens his arms to embrace the truth of our lives?

It is Jesus who teaches us to pray. Rowan Williams describes Jesus' own prayer at the time of his temptation in the desert:

> Jesus in the desert . . . looks towards God and there's nothing there that will solve a problem, nothing there that will sweep away all the questions. What there is is truth and love and patience and endless welcome. In due course that will transform us, it will bring us to joy, it will make our problems . . . fade away. But first of all we have to get used to a new climate, we have to breathe a new air, . . . the air of the Holy Spirit . . . [we have to] get used to the idea of God quite different from what we expected and yet at the same time ringing bells with what we most care about and most deeply long for.[32]

An unconditional witness with no interest to pursue, no selfhood to defend. Truth and love and patience and endless welcome. Loving God involves getting used to a new climate, breathing a new air—the air of the Holy Spirit, the Holy Spirit in which Jesus prayed and which Jesus promised us God longs to give.

Head for home, home in God. Do anything to get there. It may be that we think we've failed at our vocation of loving God and loving neighbour, but it doesn't matter. Remember the stories of the son and the manager who squandered their property. Jesus in those stories affirmed their heading for home by the strangest of means. Head for home, for we'll find there a table, a welcome, healing, stories to be told, a place to tell our stories. And we'll find forgiveness too. Forgiveness for the way we've made a mess at times of the loving of God and neighbour.

We'll find forgiveness there. We haven't heard that story yet. That story is to come. For it is in Luke's Gospel that we will hear Jesus say on the cross, "Father forgive them, for they do not know what they are doing". We will hear these words in Holy Week and on Good Friday, in the story of the crucifixion and in the extraordinary story of Easter, the stories of God's redemption of all things in Christ—the story of God's bringing all creation home.

PART 6

The Jesus Narrative

CHAPTER 24

Whisperings of Poets and Prophets

Today, the First Sunday of Advent, we hear the voice of the prophet Jeremiah. Advent is a time for hearing the voice of the prophets, for sitting with that voice. It is a voice of poetry. There is nothing logical or certain in the voice of the prophet. But the voice of poetry creates possibility, the possibility of hope, the radical possibility of God.

God speaks through Jeremiah:

> The days are surely coming, says the Lord, when I will fulfil the promise I made to the house of Israel and the house of Judah. In those days and at that time I will cause a righteous Branch to spring up for David; and he shall execute justice and righteousness in the land. In those days Judah will be saved and Jerusalem will live in safety.
>
> Jeremiah 33:14–16

Jeremiah writes in the time of exile, a time of great loss. The certainty of the world centred for the people of Judah in Jerusalem, city of king and temple, has been shattered. There is only loss and displacement. The people are exiled from home in Babylon, and there, the prophet Jeremiah speaks an uncomfortable truth, a staggered truth, a truth of loss, and then a truth of hope. The prophet Jeremiah weeps for the city of Jerusalem and the stubborn and foolish inhabitants who betrayed their God. Jeremiah places right at the feet of those people responsibility for their fate:

> Hear the word of the Lord, O house of Jacob, and all the families of the house of Israel. Thus says the Lord:
> What wrong did your ancestors find in me

> that they went far from me,
> and went after worthless things, and
> became worthless themselves?
>
> *Jeremiah 2:4-5*

Right at the heart of the place of loss, then, Jeremiah speaks another word of poetry, a word of hope. "The days are surely coming . . . The days are surely coming, when I will fulfil the promise I made," says the Lord. The longing of God in these words is palpable.

The Old Testament scholar Walter Brueggemann writes about the prophet Jeremiah: "Jeremiah's language is free, porous and impressionistic—he is a poet. . . . Poets have no advice to give people. They only want people to see differently, to re-envision life. They are not coercive. They only try to stimulate, surprise, hint, and give nuance, not more. They cannot do more, because they are making available a world that does not yet exist beyond their imagination . . . "[33] In other words: prophets do not tell us what to do. They paint a picture of a different world.

Walter Brueggemann expresses great faith in the power of *utterance*. He describes the voice of longing of those waiting in exile, those, perhaps, waiting in churches and cathedrals this First Sunday in Advent: "Is there any word from the Lord?' (Jeremiah 37:17). We reach out, in fear and hope, to be addressed by newness, because we know the human spirit will wither if there is no address."[34] The prophet Jeremiah speaks: "at that time I will cause a righteous Branch to spring up". Brueggemann reflects: "This is indeed a word from the outside . . . a word that comes in the way of poetry, that offers no explanation, no certainty, . . . It is a moment of utterance! . . . everything has now been changed by the poetic utterance, because the *poetry cannot be unsaid* . . . The word has been uttered and there is a whisper of an alternative world in the air."[35]

When the poet prophet utters a word of hope; when the voice of the prophet proclaims the presence of God, speaks comfort in the voice of God, that utterance has power. That utterance has the power to give hope. And that utterance cannot be washed away, *cannot be unsaid*. That utterance *exists* and so "everything has now been changed".

Brueggemann also notes, "Every centre of power fears poets, because poets never fight fair".[36] Poets don't use logic. Poets don't use persuasion. Unlike many centres of power, poets certainly don't use guns.

The greatest poet, the Son of God, certainly did not "fight fair". He, at times, even used silence.

Our Gospel reading from Luke 21 has the one who speaks *and is* the Word of God, using that subversive literary form, poetry:

> There will be signs in the sun, the moon, and the stars, and on the earth distress among nations confused by the roaring of the sea and the waves. People will faint from fear and foreboding of what is coming upon the world, for the powers of the heavens will be shaken. Then they will see "the Son of Man coming in a cloud" with power and great glory. Now when these things begin to take place, stand up and raise your heads, because your redemption is drawing near.
>
> Luke 21:25–8

Does our world feel a little like this, at this time? Are we fainting from fear and foreboding at the violence that has taken place in the world, in recent weeks, at the bushfires that have brought such devastation to people who live just kilometres away, in recent days? Could we imagine ourselves standing up and raising our heads? Might we possibly believe that at this time, as in so many times of struggle in world history, redemption is near?

Prophets, poets, come in many guises. In Paris at the scene of the Bataclan attacks, social media showed a reporter interviewing a father and his little boy gazing at the sea of flower tributes.

"Do you understand what happened?" the reporter asked the little boy. "Do you understand why people did that?"

"Because they are really, really mean," the little boy said. "Bad guys are not very nice." "And," he said to his father particularly, "we have to be really careful, because we have to change houses."

"Oh no, don't worry, we don't have to move out," said the little boy's father, "France is our home."

"Yes," said the little boy, "but there's bad guys everywhere. They have guns. They can shoot because they are really mean, Daddy."

"It's OK," said the Dad, "they might have guns, but we have flowers."

"But flowers don't do anything. They're for . . . They're for . . . "

"Of course they do . . . Look," said the father, "everyone's putting flowers. It's to fight against guns."

"It's to protect?" asked the little boy.

"Exactly."

"And the candles too?" asked the little boy.

"It's to remember the people who are gone yesterday," said his father.

"The flowers and the candles are here to protect us?"

"Yes."

"Do you feel better now?" said the little boy.

"Yes, I feel better."

"Everyone's putting flowers. It's to fight against guns."

Comfort for a little boy? Or could this possibly be the voice of God?

"Comfort, comfort ye my people," said a different prophet, the prophet Isaiah, to a people displaced from home.

It's not about proof, do you see? It's not about evidence. It's not about reasoned argument. It's about whispers from another world, *our* world known as made and loved by God.

Yes, prophets speak a different truth.

"The days are surely coming, says the Lord [through the prophet Jeremiah], when I will fulfil the promise I made . . . and [all] will live in safety."

"Everyone's putting flowers. It's to fight against guns."

Said a father to his little boy, beside a scene of carnage in Paris.

CHAPTER 25

I'll ride with you

It's not often that I quote politicians in a sermon. But the following words, spoken by Prime Minister Malcolm Turnbull after he attended a memorial service for the victims of the Sydney siege, seemed to capture something that we might want to ponder this morning. With his voice breaking, Malcolm Turnbull said this:

> I was on a train this morning, and you could feel the numbness in the carriage. Everyone was thinking the same thoughts: shock, horror, imagining how those people suffered during that terrible night. Thinking about the courage of the two young people that were killed.
>
> And yet I feel that everyone was also filled with love. There was something of determination on that train; a determined love; a recognition that it's love for each other; it's love for our country which binds us together and makes us the most successful, harmonious society in the world.
>
> I felt that there was, as the train rattled across the Harbour Bridge, I felt that there was a quiet determination that we weren't going to be intimidated by such hatred.
>
> I thought today's service was so beautiful. Because it was all about love. It was about that love, that love of God . . . the loving example of Jesus that should inspire us all not to be corrupted by hatred and violence, and to remain united as Australians, now and forever.

These words were spoken on the day we witnessed such terrible events in Sydney. These words were also spoken on the very day that a brutal attack on a school in Pakistan killed 148 people, most of them children.

These events are not about, or of, politics—those who work in and think about the world through political eyes were united in shock and horror at this. These events are not about religion; people of faith—and differing faiths—were united on their knees in prayer at this. These events are about the worst that human beings can do, and be, and about the best that human beings can do, and be. These events reveal the darkest places of the human heart, and they bring to light the love, the grace and the courage that may be found in the human heart. They bring to light the human capacity for what Malcolm Turnbull referred to as "determined love".

On the day of the Sydney siege, we saw the attempt to exploit social media for evil, and we saw social media empowered for good. We saw a hash tag that said "I'll ride with you"—a message to those in the Muslim community who might feel anxious about going about their daily tasks in public after the violent events in Sydney. It was a message to any one of us who felt that same anxiety, anyone who felt threatened by virtue of their race or religion or gender, the message: "You are not alone. Someone will ride with you." The message of determined love.

It seems utterly fitting that in our churches, this Advent morning, when we struggle with finding a way of living determined love, that we find ourselves reflecting on the story of the annunciation. This story tells of a young girl, Mary, who finds herself encountering an angel, Gabriel. Mary is often portrayed as a gentle person, but I do not think this is so. What God asked of her was dangerous.

They probably would have stoned her, you know. That was the punishment for adultery and her assent to God's request may well have been viewed in a similar light. Remember the woman caught in adultery, and how they asked Jesus what to do—do you remember?

> Teacher [the scribes and the Pharisees said], this woman was caught in the very act of committing adultery. Now in the law

Moses commanded us to stone such women. Now what do you say?

John 8:4–5

Did Jesus think of his mother, Mary, as he looked at the woman standing before him that day? Did he shudder at the memory of his mother's courage? Did he thank God that Joseph heard the angel's voice in the dream telling him to stand by her?

Gabriel was busy in those days. What God wanted was so huge that it needed a heavy-duty messenger to get the request across:

> In the sixth month the angel Gabriel was sent by God to a town in Galilee called Nazareth, to a virgin engaged to a man whose name was Joseph, of the house of David. The virgin's name was Mary. And he came to her and said, "Greetings, favoured one! The Lord is with you". But she was much perplexed by his words and pondered what sort of greeting this might be.
>
> *Luke 1:26–9*

The thing we must understand about Mary is that she is not gentle, she is not passive. Her life was arranged for her—she was to marry a good man—and Gabriel interrupted that life. His conversation with her was extraordinary, almost impossible to understand.

"Greetings, favoured one! The Lord is with you."

What is going on here?

The word pondered means "gave weight to". Gabriel is treated with utmost seriousness. And while we might think from the number of paintings we have seen of this Annunciation scene that it is obvious Mary would take Gabriel seriously, I would challenge that. Angels are, in fact, easy to dismiss, to turn one's back on. But Mary doesn't do this. She has a sense of God. She suspects the Lord is with her. And she's frightened. We know that because Gabriel knew it. He told her not to be afraid:

> "Do not be afraid, Mary, for you have found favour with God. And now, you will conceive in your womb and bear a son, and you will name him Jesus. He will be great, and will be called the

Son of the Most High, and the Lord God will give to him the throne of his ancestor David. He will reign over the house of Jacob forever, and of his kingdom there will be no end."

Luke 1:30–3

The request is impossible, and Mary says so. She may be frightened but it doesn't stop her from continuing to wrestle with the angel. With confronting honesty, she engages with him.

"How can this be, since I am a virgin?" (Luke 1:34).

Gabriel's answer is unlikely to help Mary greatly. He is simply asserting what Mary was already suspecting, which is that God is doing this. God is directing this conversation, and God will enable this conception to take place:

"The Holy Spirit will come upon you, and the power of the Most High will overshadow you; therefore the child to be born will be holy; he will be called Son of God."

Luke 1:35

What Mary thought was impossible, Gabriel names as possible. "Nothing is impossible with God," he says. Except that God cannot do this alone. God needs Mary. And he needs her just as she is. The one who, although frightened, does not run away. The one who, although puzzled, is not put off by something she doesn't understand. The one who suspects God is in Gabriel and who battles on until that is made clear.

God asks of Mary a profound question: "Will you bear my love to the world?" A love that we believe will redeem the world. Like Mary, we might wonder how this can be, especially in the light of events like the Sydney siege. Like Mary, we may well be almost too afraid to allow the possibility. But she does allow it.

And so she responds—a response of determined love:

"Here am I, the servant of the Lord; let it be with me according to your word."

Luke 1:38

A friend of mine told me that on Tuesday morning she went into a cafe on her way to work to buy a cup of coffee. She went into that cafe, as she did every day of her working week. The cafe owner looked at my friend, as he handed her a cup of coffee, and said, "Thank you". My friend said she looked a little puzzled at this. The owner continued: "Thank you for buying a cup of coffee."

How do we live in a world where ordinary life can, without warning, be so invaded by terror and threat? How can we live in a world where innocent children are killed as they go about their business at school? How do we live in a world, this world, where human hearts are capable of such evil and yet such good?

Scripture gives us stories to place alongside impossible questions and today's story—that of the Annunciation—is no exception. God sends Gabriel to us, as God sent Gabriel to Mary, to bid us not to be afraid—not to be afraid as God asks us to bear God's love to the world. God's very being is about bearing love, but God cannot do this alone.

There's one thing we need to remember, though. God promises us one most profound thing. This promise is found in the word Emmanuel which means "God with us". God says "You won't do this alone, you know, this bearing of love. I don't ask you to do this alone. I'll ride with you."

CHAPTER 26

Nativity—A Story Hanging in the Air

I love the nativity story. In recent days, we've heard it, read it, sung it, gazed at it. We've gathered with family and friends around that story and the presents and feasting we do to remember it. We belong in a world that celebrates Christmas—and yet doesn't—but this world is no different from the one in which Christ was born. The point about the beautiful nativity scene, I think, is that woven together there are images of God and images of earth. Angels and stars and wise men bearing gifts heavy with meaning are in the midst of a stable with sheep and cattle and a tired mother and father who gaze on their newborn child. All in a stable as there was no room for them indoors. No, the world was no different then. And all this weaving of earthly things and heavenly things seems to tell us that then, and now, and at all times, God is deeply in love with this earthly place. And God will move heaven and earth to find us and tell us about that love. And God will keep searching for us, even when we seem deaf to his approach.

Yes, we belong in a world that celebrates Christmas and yet doesn't—as at all times and in all places—God calls and creates and is born. And yet we barely see, we barely hear—for the struggle of being a human being can overwhelm us at times, all of us, even those of us who make the pilgrimage to church each week. But God keeps searching for us. The nativity story and all the stories of God are not laid to rest with the tree and the decorations as we tidy up for our summer holidays. Those stories hang in the air. They beckon to us, they whisper to us, and, just possibly, they might sustain us.

Jesus knew that. Even as a child.

The Gospel of Luke spends much time on the Infancy Narratives, the stories of John the Baptist's and Jesus' birth. The Angel Gabriel has been busy. He visits Zechariah, and he visits Mary, and he announces two births, both of them surprising and demanding of faith. Faith is offered in different ways. Canticles are sung by Mary when she meets Elizabeth, and by Zechariah when John is born and both of them point to a God who is turning the world upside down, who is bringing salvation to creation in unexpected ways. The second chapter of Luke opens with a brief account of Jesus' birth. And then the angel choir sings to the shepherds, and they travel to the Bethlehem stable to see the child who they are told will be the Messiah and Saviour. The shepherds tell Mary and Joseph what they have been told about the child, and "Mary treasured all these words and pondered them in her heart" (Luke 2:19). This was not to be the only time that Jesus' mother found herself pondering, wondering about the child to whom she had given birth and about what her life would entail in being his mother.

When Jesus is eight days old, he is circumcised and named, and at the appropriate time he is taken to the temple and prayers are said and offerings made. Again, Mary finds herself reflecting in amazement about her son, when Simeon and Anna make their pronouncements about Jesus.

Jesus, Luke tells us, "grew and became strong, filled with wisdom; and the favour of God was upon him" (Luke 2:40). What does it look like, being filled with wisdom? What signs are there even in his youth that he knows the ways of God? There is only one more thing we are told about Jesus' childhood and that comes in the snippet of story we heard read this morning:

> Now every year his parents went to Jerusalem for the festival of the Passover. And when he was twelve years old, they went up as usual for the festival. When the festival was ended and they started to return, the boy Jesus stayed behind in Jerusalem, but his parents did not know it.
>
> *Luke 2:41–3*

It is a typical scene between parents and their child. The parents are anxious. This child, though, is pushing the boundaries in an unusual way:

> After three days they found him in the temple, sitting among the teachers, listening to them and asking them questions. And all who heard him were amazed at his understanding and his answers. When his parents saw him they were astonished; and his mother said to him, "Child, why have you treated us like this? Look, your father and I have been searching for you in great anxiety." He said to them, "Why were you searching for me? Did you not know that I must be in my Father's house?"
>
> Luke 2:46–9

He knew about the stories, the scripture stories hanging in the air. He knew about spending time with them, hearing them and wrestling with them, asking questions of them and pondering and giving his own thoughts about them. He knew that the temple, the house of God, was where he belonged and that dwelling in the stories of scripture was where God is to be found. He knew about spending time with those who would do the same:

> "Why were you searching for me? Did you not know that I must be in my Father's house?"

Even at the age of twelve, he knew where he belonged and where life was to be found. And God sent him to give us that same knowledge. The knowledge of salvation.

Zechariah, in his canticle which we know as the *Benedictus*, the song he sang when his son John was born, sang of John giving the people "knowledge of salvation by the forgiveness of their sins". He beautifully sings on, "By the tender mercy of our God, the dawn from on high will break upon us, to give light to those who sit in darkness and the shadow of death, to guide our way into the way of peace" (Luke 1:77–9).

We belong in a world that celebrates Christmas—and yet doesn't. But as at any time in history, the dawn from on high continues to break upon our world, on a world where peace seems to evade us, on a world where we are only just beginning to understand the peril with which the planet which is our home is faced, on a world where we ordinary people find ourselves worrying about the ones we love dearly or the ones we miss.

The dawn from on high breaks upon us in the life and the death and the resurrection of this one whose birth we remember this week. The dawn from on high breaks upon us when our living is blessed by his spirit, the spirit of the one who knew, even as a child, that life is found in God's house, treasuring the stories of that God, pondering them, letting them infuse his life.

CHAPTER 27

Space for Our Souls

Why did he go there? Why did the Spirit lead him into the desert?

"This is my Son, the Beloved," God says to Jesus as he is baptized in the River Jordan by John. "My Son with whom I am well pleased." "My Son, the Beloved."

With God, his Father's, words ringing in his ears, this Son is led by the Spirit into the wilderness to be tempted by the devil. Jesus spends forty days there, fasting until he is famished. Then the tempter, the devil, speaks with Jesus. In the heavenly court in the Jewish scriptures, the devil, the Satan, is the accuser, the heavenly barrister, if you like, who puts suspected offenders to the test. We might imagine this devil, this tempter, as the voice inside us that doubts God's naming of us. The devil takes the name given to Jesus by God and works with it, undermines it, attempts to poison it. "If you are the Son of God," this devil says. And he lays before Jesus the three great temptations for the one who is God's Son. What does it mean to be the Son of God? Does it not mean being physically full, physically safe and politically powerful?

"Work a little magic, why don't you?" This devil hints that surely God's Son can intervene a little in nature's processes. Don't let yourself be vulnerable, powerless. Surely the Son of God has extraordinary power?

For reasons that the devil cannot possibly understand, Jesus has come into the desert, and has spent forty days and forty nights allowing his humanity, his physical being, to be placed under extreme pressure. Jesus allows himself to be vulnerable, to be powerless. Jesus is famished. He is embracing his humanity and the frailty that human beings can know, firstly in a physical way.

Physically diminished, Jesus then faces the *spiritual* frailty of a human being. Temptation—to shortcut what it is to be a child of God. Temptation—to risk one's soul. This is the devil's specialty.

"If you are the Son of God, command these stones to become loaves of bread." The devil says: Work a little magic to heal your hunger.

Jesus responds to each temptation with words of scripture, each time from the book Deuteronomy, one of the books of the Law:

> It is written, [says Jesus],
> "One does not live by bread alone,
> but by every word that comes from the mouth of God".
> *Matthew 4:3–4*

Jesus puts physical hunger in its place—our true food is the spiritual sustenance that comes from God. The forty days and forty nights that Jesus spends in the wilderness remind us, of course, of the time the Israelites spent in the wilderness as they were led by Moses from slavery in Egypt to freedom in the promised land. Those Israelites cried out to God the moment they became hungry and God gave them manna—the food that was supplied each day and only enough for the day—and so the people were not only fed, but taught dependence on God. Jesus knows and responds out of his dependence on God. It is the love and presence of God that sustains him.

The devil then takes Jesus to Jerusalem and placing him on the pinnacle of the temple, says to him, "If you are the Son of God, throw yourself down; for it is written, 'He will command his angels concerning you', and 'On their hands they will bear you up, so that you will not dash your foot against a stone'" (Matthew 4:6).

The devil, we notice, has decided that if Jesus is arguing using the words of scripture, then he can match Jesus at that game. Jesus and the devil are working in a manner not unlike Jewish rabbis, wrestling with scripture to discern the truth of God's ways. This temptation is about taking a risk, about gambling. The devil is tempting Jesus to take the greatest gamble of all, with his life.

Jesus quotes scripture back at the devil, "Again it is written, 'Do not put the Lord your God to the test'" (Matthew 4:7).

Here Jesus is tempted to put himself, and his identity as God's Son, on show, to draw attention to himself, to place himself in danger. We know all too well that Jesus will place himself in danger, danger that costs him his life, when he has done his work on earth. Jesus will go to his passion and death, dying as he lives, sustained by his profound faith and trust in God. And God does not rescue him.

Finally, in the third temptation, the devil takes Jesus to a very high mountain and shows him all the kingdoms of the world and their splendour; and he says to him, "All these I will give you, if you will fall down and worship me". Jesus says to him, "Away with you, Satan! for it is written, 'Worship the Lord your God, and serve only him'" (Matthew 4:9–10).

The devil does not bother to remind Jesus that he is the Son of God in this final temptation. This is about the worship of another god. This, surely the most sinister of the three temptations, again mirrors the failure of the Israelites in the wilderness to behave well as people of God. Becoming impatient with the God who had promised to lead them to freedom, they made a golden calf and worshipped that instead. The devil promises Jesus all earthly power, all the kingdoms of the world, if he will turn away from his worship of his Father. But Jesus' kingdom is not of this world. His love is only for God.

Jesus, in the wilderness, embraces his humanity. As he faces temptation, he allows only his humanity, and his deep trust in his Father's love, to support him. Jesus lives and loves, and he will die and rise again, with only his humanity and his faith in that Father's love. This time in the wilderness is a time of wrestling with what it is to be a human being who is named God's Beloved Son.

Lent might be, for us, a time of similar wrestling, reflecting. What is it to be a human being who is God's beloved child? What does it mean for us to be children of God?

Why would we go to the desert?

Why did Jesus go?

The word salvation is derived from a Hebrew word which means "to be spacious". Jesus' time of temptation in the wilderness might be thought of as a time for making space. Perhaps Lent is a time for making space. A time for reflecting on what it is that we think feeds us, makes us worthwhile, that is not God, and fasting from that for a while. What might it be that makes us feel better, feel worthwhile. It could be alcohol or chocolate, the traditional Lenten fasts, but it might be many other things. It is because we are God's beloved child that we are worthwhile. What gets in the way of that?

And pondering Jesus' second temptation, we might wonder when it is that we gamble, what it is that we place at risk? Might we reflect upon that? Do we place at risk our health, our most precious relationships, our families, our friends? Do we gamble with our souls?

And the third temptation that Jesus wrestled with was idolatry. What do we worship? We all have idols, for loving God is difficult. What do we love in place of God? What do we find easier to love?

The word salvation is about making space, space for our souls. For our forty days and forty nights might we find a way to do that? Might we find a few minutes each day to sit quietly and hear God's voice naming us beloved? And might we wonder about what it is that muffles that voice, what makes us doubt that we could be so named? What are our sins? And do we believe them forgiven? Which of God's gifts to us do we place at risk?

Jesus went to the desert and faced temptation and then lived his earthly life with only his humanity and the great love of God. We, too, have our humanity and the great love of God. Might this Lent be a time to make space for that, for pondering the blessing and struggle of being named God's beloved ones?

CHAPTER 28

Behold the Wood of the Cross

"Behold the wood of the cross, behold the wood of the cross on which hangs the Saviour of the world."

I wonder if it would not be better if we sat in silence. We have heard the choir sing from the balcony, their anthems about the faithfulness of this cross. We have heard the Passion read from John's Gospel. We have one another's company in which to encounter the silence, after all. We have wood and stone, fabric and glass in which the story is told, surrounding us in our cathedral. Might we not sit and contemplate, allowing the stories of our lives, with their sins and their frailties, to be encountered by this wild truth, that Jesus of Nazareth died that we might know the fiery and unquenchable, forgiving and enabling, love of God. Might we not sit in silence?

Only Jesus spoke. He was pretty well silent through his trial but on the cross he spoke. Seven Last Words as tradition has it, these seven words garnered from the Gospels, none of them containing all the words. As he hung dying on his cross, Jesus spoke. And so this Good Friday morning we will ponder three of the things he said.

Jesus' first and final words begin with him addressing his Father: "Father, forgive them for they do not know what they are doing" (Luke 23:34), Jesus says, as he gazes upon the ones who have nailed him to the cross. A lot of unhelpful things are said about the way in which, in Jesus' crucifixion, God takes away the sins of the world. God gave his Son, people say. But this is not a transaction in the heavenly realm. Not some sort of prisoner exchange. Jesus' life handed over that our lives might be handed back. That's not what is going on here.

Michael Mayne, the former Dean of Westminster Abbey, in his Lent book, *Dust that Dreams of Glory*, puts it this way:

> Let me tell you what [Jesus' death] does not mean, for over the centuries there have been some strange and distorting theories about the sacrificial death of Christ. It does not mean that God sent an innocent man to death because he requires blood. The Passion and death of Jesus are not a pagan sacrifice. It does not mean Jesus came to placate an angry God, nor to show us how we must submit to an inscrutable God . . . Jesus came to do one thing: to embody the love of God for his creation.[37]

"Father, forgive them for they do not know what they are doing," Jesus says, as he gazes upon the ones who have nailed him to the cross. And he remembers Judas who betrayed him, and Peter who promised to follow him but denied him, and all the others who have fled in terror. Jesus looks at the men before him and, in pain and agony and with his few final breaths, he forgives them. And as he forgives them, he forgives us all. All the petty betrayals and denials and all the violence and jealousies. He forgives them all. And then, when the resurrection comes in all its mystery, and the crucified Jesus stands with the marks of the nails in his hands and the mark of the spear in his side, when he comes and speaks his words of peace and he breathes his spirit on creation, it is the spirit of the one who dying forgave, dying forgives. The spirit of Christ is the spirit of forgiveness. This is something of the way in which God, in Jesus' death, forgives the sins of the world.

He has been so close to his Father. He called his father Abba, the word a little child would use as he snuggled onto their utterly trusted parent's lap. Jesus lived and breathed, loved and healed, taught and set free, those who he encountered in his three short years of ministry, out of that deep closeness to God.

On the cross that closeness is gone. Probably for the first time in his life, he feels abandoned.

"My God, My God, why have you forsaken me?" he says (Mark 15:34). Jesus here embraces human despair, human terror. Jesus hangs in solidarity with all who have felt abandoned by God. Jesus knows acute physical suffering and the terrible mental and spiritual suffering that can accompany it. Jesus endures what we endure, chooses to endure what we endure when terror and pain wrenches us apart and we have nothing to which we can cling. And where is the loving Father? What is happening in the life of God? Has God the Father abandoned God the Son? I don't think so.

It is as if the Father is standing helpless at a distance, for comfort cannot be allowed here. It is as if the Father suffers the Son's dying as the Son suffers the Father's absence in his death. It is as if there is anguish in the very heart of God, as if the heart of the Trinity is broken. The very being of God endures brokenness, that the world might be redeemed.[38]

"My God, My God, why have you forsaken me?" Jesus says.

Michael Mayne says:

> What Good Friday does is invite us once again to open ourselves to the God who doesn't answer our Job-like questions about the "Why?" of evil and pain and suffering: instead he enters into the heart of the questions himself. The crucified Jesus is the only accurate picture of God the world has ever seen.[39]

This picture is mirrored across time and place where in human and created life the question "Why?" is cried out.

On 14 February 2018, Valentine's Day, in Marjory Stoneman Douglas High School in Parkland, Florida, a student gunman killed seventeen students in the deadliest high school shooting in the country's history.

A newspaper report stated: "Just a month later, thousands of students poured out of classrooms in the United States on Wednesday 14th March in an unprecedented expression of mourning and a demand for action to stem the country's epidemic of gun violence."

In a stunning visual riposte to the public inertia that has followed mass shootings in the US, crowds of students at an estimated 3,000 schools across the country marched on running tracks, through car parks and around building perimeters, carrying signs that read "Enough".[40]

Enough.

And then there is the cry from the natural world:

Each one of us has seen pictures in social and news media of whales with their stomachs choking in plastic bags, of birds with their stomachs filled with tiny pieces of coloured plastic that they are enticed into believing is food. Are these sea creatures, these birds, created and beloved by God, crying out "Why?" to our neglect of them? Crying out "Enough" to those of us who have caused this neglect? Is Jesus in solidarity with these dying creatures on his cross?

The well-known Cambridge physicist Stephen Hawking suffered from what is surely one of the cruellest diseases that a human being can endure, motor neurone disease. He died on 14 March 2018, aged seventy-six. His biographer described the scene in his university office over twenty years before:

> The figure in the [physics students'] midst is pitiful by all normal standards, . . . He wears a bib, and a nurse holds his forehead and tips his head forward so that he can drink his tea out of the cup she holds under his chin. His hair is tousled, his mouth is slack, and his eyes are weary over the eyeglasses that have slipped down his nose a little. But at a disrespectful [joke] from one of his students his face breaks into a grin that would light up the universe.[41]

A broken body shot through with redeeming life.

Like this broken body, the one who hangs before us. This Jesus who stands alongside students grieving their dead friends and crying "Enough" about gun violence. This Jesus who stands alongside whales and sea birds choking on plastic, their broken bodies crying out to us "When will you see?" about the damage caused by plastic waste on our planet. This Jesus who stands alongside those, like Stephen Hawking, who suffer the cruellest of diseases. All of us, in our different ways, broken but shot through with redeeming life because Jesus died in this way so we might know that he enters into the heart of the questions himself. Yes. The crucified Jesus is the only accurate picture of God the world has ever seen. And our redemption is found there.

Jesus' final word on the cross is again addressed to his Father:

> "Father, into your hands I commend my spirit."
>
> *Luke 23:46*

Jesus first and final words are spoken to the one in whom he lived his life, his Abba, his Father.

A Jewish child, Jesus would have said his prayers before he went to sleep. The prayer at night-time came from Psalm 31: "Into your hand I commit my spirit." As he dies, Jesus prays. He has prayed for forgiveness, a forgiveness that sends ripples throughout creation and restores us whatever we have done, of whatever we are ashamed; he has endured and prayed in his abandonment that we might know he is alongside us and brings healing in all our pain and suffering and loneliness; and now with his final breath, his final word, he shows us how to die. When his work is accomplished, when our work is accomplished, there is only one thing to do. Only one more word to speak. And that is to pray one last prayer. The night prayer. The prayer of utter trust:

"Father, into your hands I commend my spirit."

This is God. This is what God looks like.

"Behold the wood of the cross; behold the wood of the cross on which hangs the Saviour of the world."

CHAPTER 29

Was it watching Notre Dame burn?

Was it watching Notre Dame burn? Was that the closest that death and destruction and the truth of the utter vulnerability of our life came to us in recent days?

Flames and smoke rose from the blaze at Notre Dame Cathedral in Paris that night. The Cathedral was within "fifteen to thirty minutes" of complete destruction as firefighters battled to stop flames reaching its gothic bell towers, French authorities revealed.

Was it watching Notre Dame burn? Was it when the spire fell almost in slow motion to the gasps and cries of Parisians who found in this building some sense of hope, of meaning, of identity? Was it watching Notre Dame burn that our vulnerability struck us?

Or was it listening to the sixteen-year-old Swedish climate activist Greta Thunberg addressing the European Union Council about the desperate state of our planet? As she spoke of a "sixth mass extinction", her voice faltered. "The extinction rate is up to six times faster than what is considered normal, with up to 200 species becoming extinct every single day," she said. "Erosion of fertile topsoil, deforestation of the rainforest, toxic air pollution, loss of insects and wildlife, acidification of our oceans—these are all disastrous trends.... It is still not too late to act. It will take a far-reaching vision, it will take courage, it will take fierce, fierce determination to act now, to lay the foundations where we may not know all the details about how to shape the ceiling," she said. "In other words, it will take cathedral thinking. I ask you to please wake up and make changes required possible."[42]

Is it when we contemplate our deep concern for our planet that we find ourselves remembering those women walking to the tomb, to Jesus' tomb?

Or have we known our own deaths in recent days? Have we sat beside the coffins of our own loved ones and known the utter loneliness that comes from the truth that we will not talk with them any more, drink a cup of tea with them any more, be irritated by them any more, love their very presence any more? Here in our cathedral community we have lost several people dear to us in recent weeks and we know that biting loneliness, that fierce truth. The truth that death is.

We cannot hear this story of Jesus' empty tomb and what happened there, we cannot hear *this* story unless we have sat by the tombs of defeat and loneliness, known what it is to be human beings who lose what we love and hold dear. This is the place where our Gospel story belongs.

He was their hope, their meaning, their identity. And on Good Friday, Golgotha hurled death at him. Jesus' death was bitter and cruel, a place of torture and mockery, of desertion and betrayal. And he, even knowing the despair of his Father God's absence in it, had loved and forgiven, with a forgiveness that sent shock waves through creation. "Father, forgive them," he said looking at the ones who had nailed him to his cross, "for they do not know what they are doing." And then as he died, he still trusted God. "Father, into your hands I commit my spirit", he said as he breathed his final breath. Jesus inhabited death, all the fear and pain of it, all the senselessness of it, for us.

They wrapped his body in linen cloths and placed him in a tomb:

> Early on the first day of the week, while it is still dark, Mary Magdalene came to the tomb and saw that the stone had been removed from the tomb. So she ran and went to Simon Peter and the other disciple, the one whom Jesus loved, and said to them, "They have taken the Lord out of the tomb, and we do not know where they have laid him".
>
> *John 20:1–2*

Mary Magdalene has come to Jesus' tomb to spend a little more time with him, with the truth of his death. But the tomb is empty. The linen cloths are lying there, folded, but Jesus is gone. Simon Peter and the other disciple run to the tomb when Mary has told them what she has seen, and they look inside. It is the other disciple who this story says "saw and believed", saw and believed that life has emerged here, that Jesus has risen from the dead, as he said he would.

So far all we have is a lack of him, a lack of death, and the faith of this disciple, but Mary stays, weeping. As she weeps, she bends over to look into the tomb; and she sees two angels in white, who ask her why she is weeping. She says to them, "They have taken away my Lord, and I do not know where they have laid him". Then she turns round and sees Jesus standing there, but she does not know that it is him. How is it possible that she doesn't know Jesus? How could she not know him? "Jesus said to her, 'Woman, why are you weeping? For whom are you looking?' Supposing him to be the gardener, she said to him, 'Sir, if you have carried him away, tell me where you have laid him, and I will take him away'. Jesus said to her, 'Mary!'" (John 20:11–16).

Twice, she is asked why she is weeping. It is as if the ones who know God's way of things, the angels, Jesus himself, know that tears have no place here. A tomb where tears absolutely have a place has been transformed. "Woman, why are you weeping?" Mary assumes the one speaking to her is a gardener and that the body, the evidence that this is still a place of death, has just been placed somewhere else. It is when Jesus speaks her name that she knows him. "Mary," he says. The one who gave her hope and healing, identity and meaning is restored to her in the speaking of her name. Their relationship is restored.

God's life has broken in here. This is an extraordinary truth, this truth of resurrection. It is not some sweet story. It is a wild and utterly unexpected truth, that this faithful man who endured this awful death has been vindicated by God. Your will be done, Jesus said in that other garden, the Gethsemane Garden, as he faced what lay ahead. And this is God's will. We see it now, he lives it now, *he lives*. God's will, even in death, is about life.

One priest, a previous canon of St Paul's Cathedral in London, Lucy Winkett, put it this way:

> Resurrection is not a metaphor for mere happiness or relief at coming through something difficult. Resurrection is what there is on the other side of nothing. It is the life we had not thought of, and despite our best efforts, will not be able to imagine.[43]

Resurrection is what there is on the other side of nothing. Death looks like nothing.

Mary knows him then, when her name is spoken. She turns and says to him in Hebrew, "Rabbouni!" (which means "teacher"). As any of us would, Mary thinks he is back and their friendship can go on as it did before. We can imagine her reaching out to hold him, to check that he is real. Jesus says to her, "Do not hold on to me". This teacher, indeed, shows her how things must be with a resurrected Lord, one that we cannot hold on to.

But beyond death, Jesus is there. All his loving, healing presence is there, looking us in the face and saying our name, teaching us how to live this new and unexpected truth.

Was it watching Notre Dame burn? Was that the closest that death and destruction and the truth of the utter vulnerability of created life has come to us? Did we see the photo inside that beautiful burnt cathedral the next morning? Did we see, amidst the ash and grey water, the cross? Did we see the light shining on the cross? Just like Jesus walking near the tomb, really. The great truth of Easter—that God's light shines where death once was. That God's love lives there, embracing us in the places of our tombs.

CHAPTER 30

Doubts and Loves Dig Up the World

We live in a world where there is much violence. We live in a world where we greatly struggle to find peace. We live in a world where we saw a man walk into a Brussels airport and blow himself up, killing scores of people and injuring many more. We live in a world where we see year after year millions made homeless, not through natural disaster but through the unnatural violence of human beings. We sit here in our cathedral knowing that the violence and fear and cowardice that can plague the human heart are our violence and fear and cowardice too.

And then we hear a story. Jesus walks into an upper room where his disciples huddle in just such fear and says to them, "Peace be with you". And we might wonder about that. The story we have heard read is set on the eighth day of Jesus' resurrection. This Second Sunday of Easter is our eighth day. We have journeyed through Holy Week with Jesus to the cross, and we have risen before dawn to witness the lighting of the new fire, and we have sung the joy of Easter. We now return to our cathedral a week later, and this Sunday we see him enter an upper room on two occasions a week apart and say to his frightened disciples, "Peace be with you".

The Roman Catholic theologian, James Alison, writes of the world having been turned upside down by God's action in the death and resurrection of Christ, who he calls a victim:

> The making of [Jesus] a victim . . . made it possible for God to be revealed for what he really is: the forgiving victim.[44]

James Alison highlights that what is set free into the world in the resurrection is the forgiving spirit of the one who was crucified, the one who, on the cross, cried out to his Father, "Father, forgive them for they do not know what they are doing". And once this spirit of forgiveness is set free in the world, it is a different place, and the way we relate to one another can be a different thing.

Jesus in the upper room has the marks of the nails in his hands and the marks of the spear in his side. He knows what it is to die a violent death and to die forgiving those who caused his death. That knowledge, that presence, is the one who speaks of and gives peace. Only one who knew violence and forgave that violence can give true peace.

The disciples heard of and knew Jesus' peace. Thomas, though, was missing.

When the other disciples told him that they had seen Jesus, he said to them, "Unless I see the mark of the nails in his hands, and put my finger in the mark of the nails and my hand in his side, I will not believe" (John 20:25). We think of Thomas as the one who asked questions, but truly the other disciples were no different. They did not believe the stories from the women of Jesus' resurrection. It was only when he appeared to them that they believed.

We all doubt. Doubt is part of faith. One scholar, Tony Kelly, seems positively to encourage our doubt, our questioning. He wrote:

> God is present at the edge of our real questions. Jesus is always a question for us. At the beginning of John's Gospel, the first words spoken by Jesus are: "What are you looking for?" (John 1:38).[45]

God is present at the edge of our real questions.

And Thomas questioned. He questioned Jesus' resurrection, and he laid down conditions for his coming to belief. And what is so very moving is that Jesus gave Thomas just what he asked for:

> A week later his disciples were again in the house, and Thomas was with them. Although the doors were shut, Jesus came and stood among them and said, "Peace be with you". Then he said to Thomas, "Put your finger here and see my hands. Reach out your hand and put it in my side. Do not doubt but believe". Thomas answered him, "My Lord and my God!"
>
> *John 20:26–8*

Jesus' words to Thomas match exactly the words spoken by Thomas. This crucified one, with the signs of his death still present in his risen body, stands and speaks his words of peace to Thomas. And what we might notice is that Thomas does not need to touch him anymore. It is not touching Jesus that brings him to faith but Jesus' presence, Jesus' gracious gift of himself. Jesus actually says in the Greek, "Do not be unbelieving but believing". Jesus' longing is that Thomas believes, that his disciples believe, that we believe. The writer of John's Gospel says at the end of this chapter that his book was written *that we might believe*. And through believing have life.

Thomas allowed his question. He spoke his truth, his unbelief, his honest doubt about the resurrection of Jesus. And Jesus honoured that unbelief. In Tony Kelly's words, God was present at the edge of his real question. Jesus gave himself to Thomas and Jesus' grace led to Thomas' confession, "My Lord and my God!" Thomas found God in the place of doubt.

A twentieth-century Israeli poet, Yehuda Amichai, wrote the following about doubt:

> From the place where we are right
> Flowers will never grow
> in the spring.
> The place where we are right
> Is hard and trampled
> like a yard.
> But doubts and loves
> dig up the world
> like a mole, a plow.
> And a whisper will be heard
> in the place where the ruined
> house once stood.[46]

Doubts and loves dig up the world like a mole, a plow.

It is interesting that doubt and love are placed alongside one another in this poem. I suppose it is another way of saying that God and questions are no strangers to one another.

In a few weeks' time we will celebrate the feast of Pentecost, and we will read the account from the Acts of the Apostles about Jesus sending the Holy Spirit. The Gospel of John tells the story a little differently. In the first scene we read about this morning, when Jesus spoke his words of peace to the disciples, Jesus also gives his spirit. This is John's Pentecost, if you like:

> Then the disciples rejoiced when they saw the Lord. Jesus said to them again, "Peace be with you. As the Father has sent me, so I send you". When he had said this, he breathed on them and said to them, "Receive the Holy Spirit. If you forgive the sins of any, they are forgiven them; if you retain the sins of any, they are retained".
>
> *John 20:20–3*

Jesus gives his disciples peace, and he sends them out into the world as the Father has sent him. And he gives his spirit, this spirit of the one who died forgiving, remember; he gives that spirit, and he tells us to forgive. And so we are sent out.

What shall we do with his words of peace ringing in our ears? Shall we serve one another as he served that Thursday night at his final supper? Shall we love as he loved that Friday when he died? Shall we wait with those who seem to be in the dead places where life is almost only a memory, as Jesus waited in the grave? Shall we, like the disciples sit with our questions, name our doubts? Shall we cry out our need for faith and what it is that might bring us to belief as Thomas did?

He sends us out . . . but he will go with us. The one with the marks of the nails in his hands, and the memory of the words of forgiveness he spoke to those who crucified him ringing in our ears, will accompany us. Jesus' gracious, forgiving, peace-bringing presence will be with us as we go to take God's love to the world.

CHAPTER 31

Turning to Christ

St Paul, in his letter to the people of Galatia, wrote the following:

> Live by the Spirit... And do not gratify the desires of the flesh.
> ... The fruit of the Spirit is love, joy, peace, patience, kindness, generosity, faithfulness, gentleness, and self-control.
> *Galatians 5:16,22,23*

As we celebrate the Feast of Pentecost, we will remind ourselves of the circumstances that prompted Paul to write his letter to the Galatians, and then we will spend a little time noticing that, contained within the portion of the letter we heard read, are two lists. Paul is encouraging us to move from one list—the list of the desires of the flesh as he calls it—towards another list—the list of the fruit of the spirit. And we will ponder the nature of the spirit, the Holy Spirit, who will support our movement from one list to another, a movement that is, effectively, one of conversion.

But, firstly, what prompted Paul to write this letter? Paul has an issue with the people of the church in Galatia, and he is not backward in letting his views be known:

> You foolish Galatians! [he writes], Who has bewitched you? It was before your eyes that Jesus Christ was publicly exhibited as crucified! The only thing I want to learn from you is this: Did you receive the Spirit by doing the works of the law or by believing what you heard? Are you so foolish? Having started with the Spirit, are you now ending with the flesh?
> *Galatians 3:1-3*

The issue is this: should those Gentiles in Galatia, who are newly converted, also abide by the Jewish Law? In particular, should these Gentile men be circumcised? Paul is horrified that these new Christians have failed to understand the key to their fledgling faith.

> We know, [Paul states], that a person is justified not by the works of the law but through faith in Jesus Christ. And we have come to believe in Christ Jesus, so that we might be justified by faith in Christ, and not by doing the works of the law, because no one will be justified by the works of the law.
>
> *Galatians 2:16*

It is faith that matters, the only thing that matters. And it is the Spirit, the Holy Spirit, whose coming we remember in our churches today, that nurtures our faith:

> But when the fullness of time had come, God sent his Son, born of a woman, born under the law, in order to redeem those who were under the law, so that we might receive adoption as children. And because you are children, God has sent the Spirit of his Son into our hearts, crying, "Abba! Father!" So you are no longer a slave but a child, and if a child then also an heir, through God.
>
> *Galatians 4:4–7*

This Spirit nurtures us in the life of children of God. No longer are we slaves to the law. The Spirit nurtures our faith in God, that through that faith we might live as those who exhibit the fruit of the Spirit that was referred to in the second list from our reading: "Live by the Spirit, I say, and do not gratify the desires of the flesh," Paul exhorts the Galatians (Galatians 5:16).

We need to spend a little time trying to understand what Paul means by living by the flesh. We need to be clear that Paul is not saying that all the things of this physical world are wrong, that all aspects of being a physical human being are wrong. Far from it. In the book of Genesis, we hear in the story of creation that God made the things of the world, and God said over and over of God's creation, "it is good". When God made humankind, "God saw everything he had made, and indeed, it was very good" (Genesis 1:31). In the incarnation, when, in Jesus of Nazareth, "the Word became flesh and lived among us" (John 1:14), God further affirms the value of the created world. So what does Paul mean? When he speaks of the flesh, he says this:

> For what the flesh desires is opposed to the Spirit, and what the Spirit desires is opposed to the flesh; for these are opposed to each other, to prevent you from doing what you want.
> *Galatians 5:17*

When Paul writes of "the flesh" he is talking about, not all physical things, but anything that is opposed to the Spirit, the spirit of Christ, the spirit of love and forgiveness. The "things of the flesh" are those things that are not about love and forgiveness.

The first list that Paul writes about, in Galatians 5, contains the sins of the flesh—"fornication, impurity, licentiousness, idolatry, sorcery, enmities, strife, jealousy, anger, quarrels, dissensions, factions, envy, drunkenness, carousing, and things like these" (Galatians 5:20-1). Put simply, this long list encompasses physical, spiritual and emotional actions that are manipulative and exploitative of another person, or even of ourselves.

The fruit of the Spirit is love, joy, peace, patience, kindness, generosity, faithfulness, gentleness, and self-control (Galatians 5:22-3). This fruit blesses the one in whom the fruit is nurtured, and anyone with whom that person relates.

What Paul desires is a process of conversion from his first list to his second. "Do you turn to Christ?" we are asked at baptism and confirmation. "Do you turn away from your sins?" This turning towards Christ and this turning away from sin, this conversion, is rarely an instant thing but is more a way of living. This turning to Christ is imaged, I think, by a plant, placed on a windowsill, growing gradually towards the sun. What nurtures that turning towards Christ and this turning away from sin? "God has sent the Spirit of his Son into our hearts, crying, 'Abba! Father!'" Paul writes to the people of Galatia (Galatians 4:6). It is the

Holy Spirit that makes its home in our hearts and helps us to know we are children of God. "Live by the Spirit," Paul goes on.

What is this Spirit like, this Holy Spirit that helps us know we are children of God, this Spirit whose coming we remember today? Over the past months we have remembered Christ's death and resurrection, and we have remembered his ascension into heaven. When he left the disciples in this strange but profound way, Jesus told the disciples to wait for the coming of the Holy Spirit.

The Catholic theologian James Alison writes about the essence of this Spirit:

> The Holy Spirit is not some vague numinous force that is somehow bigger and less exclusive than the crucified and risen Jesus—and rather nicer, perhaps, having to do with peace and joy and so on, rather than murder and violence. The Holy Spirit is the Spirit of the crucified and risen Jesus, and any joy, peace and so on that is genuinely of the Holy Spirit is essentially linked to the presence of the crucified and risen one.[47]

The Holy Spirit that is given at Pentecost is Jesus' spirit, the spirit of the one who died loving and caring for those who stood at the foot of his cross, the one who forgave those who nailed him to that cross. Love and forgiveness, the essence of the heart of God is, of course, the essence of the Holy Spirit. It is this Spirit that will nurture our conversion, our turning to Christ, our gradually being able to live by the Spirit, to be guided by the Spirit, and to show forth in our lives that Spirit's fruit.

Do you turn to Christ? Yes, God, we turn to Christ. Do you repent of your sins? Yes, God, we do repent of our sins. May the Holy Spirit bless us as we, not unlike a plant on a windowsill that gradually grows towards the sun, grow in the likeness of Christ, who made us and redeems us and gives us life.

CHAPTER 32

A Loving Community

In the last months, we have journeyed again with the story of Christ. Through Lent, we have pondered what *we* are like, what it is to be a human being, physically and spiritually frail, made, though, in the image of God, forgiven by the great love of God. When we entered Holy Week, we saw what *God* is like as we watched Jesus die, loving those courageous enough to stand at the foot of his cross, lovingly forgiving those who nailed him there. We gathered at dawn on Easter Day, to wonder again at the mystery of the resurrection, to know the God we gather to worship here as the God and Father of Christ, the God who raised Jesus from the dead. We listened to the resurrection stories, and we heard, from the Gospel of John, the story of Jesus appearing to the frightened disciples in the upper room. "Peace be with you," Jesus said, showing the disciples his hands and his side. "As the Father sent me so I send you." Then he breathed on them, and said to them, "Receive the Holy Spirit". (John 20:19–22). We pondered, on Pentecost Sunday, the idea that the word "breathed", which is used in the creation account in the book of Genesis, is closely connected to the word "breathed" used here. The writer of John's Gospel is making it quite clear that we are looking at God's *new* creation in the resurrection and the breathing of the Holy Spirit. This Spirit, the spirit of the crucified and risen Jesus, has as its heart God's heart, God's love and forgiveness.

And so today we hear the final words of Matthew's Gospel—the account of Jesus commissioning his disciples:

> Go therefore and make disciples of all nations, baptizing them
> in the name of the Father and of the Son and of the Holy Spirit,

and teaching them to obey everything that I have commanded you. And remember, I am with you always, to the end of the age.
Matthew 28:19-20

"I am with you always" is one of the key themes of the Gospel of Matthew, the one that speaks of the coming of "Emmanuel", God with us.

As we have made this journey through the story of Christ, we have lived our own story in the midst of the world in a time of great struggle. In the wake of the violence in Manchester, I stood here and spoke about Barack Obama's never wishing to address his country again about the issue of violence . . . and less than two weeks later, another burst of hatred erupted in London. We pondered the undeniable truth, that our hearts are not as big as God's heart, and so some acts of violence affect us more than others. That a nurse from our own state died in the violence in London, rushing to help others, cannot but move us. These events leave us feeling a sense of helplessness, compassion, fear and anger. But the story of God holds all these things—love and hate, peace and violence, birth and death, forgiveness and the great struggle to forgive. This is the story of the God who we are promised will be with us always.

Next week, and for week after week following on from that, we will enter the season of what is liturgically known as "ordinary" time. The colour in our cathedral, and churches across the world, will be green. We will enter the long season of the precious ordinary days, as I sometimes think of them. Before that, though, this Sunday, Trinity Sunday, we pause to wonder about something. We pause to wonder about the nature of God. What is God like? This is a question we engage with, with some trepidation.

What is God like? Baptize "in the name of the Father, of the Son and of the Holy Spirit", Jesus tells his disciples. "The grace of the Lord Jesus Christ, the love of God, and the communion of the Holy Spirit be with all of you" (2 Corinthians 13:13). Paul writes this at the close of his second letter to the people of Corinth, words that we know and say as "the Grace".

Paul could have finished his letter, "God be with you", and Jesus could have exhorted us to baptize new disciples "in the name of God", so this threefold blessing, this pointing to God as three "persons", one God, as the theologians put it, does matter. Is there anything in the idea of Trinity that can help us in our task of gathering others in and living in the great love of God? Is there any image or idea that can help us to pray when innocent people are killed going to concerts, going about their business on bridges and in markets?

When Jesus is asked what God is like, he tells stories, often parables. What is God like? "There was a man with two sons . . ."; Jesus begins the Parable of the Prodigal Son. "Who is my neighbour?" Jesus is asked. "A man went down a road to Jericho . . ."; Jesus tells the story of the Good Samaritan. One theologian, Alister McGrath, suggests that the idea of the Trinity is actually a *"story"*, a story about God, that an abstract definition for God would probably be unhelpful, but that a story tells us much. God is known through God's story.[48]

What matters a great deal is that God *wants* to be known. God reveals who God is. Jesus is sometimes described as God's self-communication—the "Word", or message if you like, from God. Jesus is sometimes called a sacrament or window into God. God is not a distant creator; God longs that we know who God is. And so the story of God, the story that is the Trinity—is told. The Father is revealed through the Son. We might well ask how we recognize this revelation. How do we see God in Jesus' life, death and resurrection? This gift of sight is the work of the Holy Spirit. The Spirit helps us know.

When we hear the story of Jesus' passion, when we hear Jesus saying, "I will be with you always", when we hear these Gospel stories and something tells us this is about God, that something is the Holy Spirit. When we see the sun setting as we walk along the beach, or we watch an ibis foraging in the parklands, or we are touched by the kindness of another human being, and these things seem to show us something of God, what moves our understanding in this way is the Holy Spirit. When a young nurse dies running to help a fellow human being on a bridge in London, it is the Holy Spirit that helps us ponder the possibility that we have been shown a glimpse of God.

How, though, do the Father, the Son and the Holy Spirit work together? The scholars warn us that these three "persons" are not three separate beings who do three separate things. What kind of understanding or image will help us here?

Another scholar, Jürgen Moltmann, describes the Trinity as a deeply loving community. This is perhaps difficult to connect with the biblical stories, but it is worth spending time with. The language of John's Gospel, where Jesus invites us to abide in God, does resonate. "You will know that I am in my Father, and you in me, and I in you," Jesus says. " . . . the Holy Spirit, whom the Father will send in my name, will teach you everything . . . " he continues (John 14:20,26). If the essence of the nature of God is loving community, human beings, and especially the Church, are encouraged to live in loving community.

The idea of the Trinity as a loving community is illustrated by a well-known icon. On the front of our orders of service this morning is an image of Rublev's Trinity, an icon created in the fifteenth century by Russian painter Andrei Rublev. The icon depicts the three angels visiting Abraham at the Oak of Mamre from Genesis 18, but it is interpreted as an image of the Trinity. What is fascinating about the three figures is the direction in which they are facing: the loving gaze from one to another, the community gathered around the table. If we gaze at the icon for a long time, we may find that we feel invited into this community of love. We might well imagine prayer as being gathered in to sit at this table. This place of love, this heart of God, is the place where we might safely bring the love and hate, peace and violence, birth and death, forgiveness and the great struggle to forgive that seem to characterize our lives.

"Go therefore," Jesus said, "and make disciples of all nations, . . . And remember, I am with you always, to the end of the age" (Matthew 28:19–20). It may be that Alister McGrath's idea of the Trinity as a story helps us. It may be that we resonate with Jürgen Moltmann's image of the Trinity as a deeply loving community. It may be that gazing at Rublev's icon is, for us, a meaningful place to be. However the reality of the nature of God as Trinity touches us, praying and resting in the community of love that is the heart of God will bless us, and will prepare us to take that love to the world.

CHAPTER 33

Bringing All Creation Home

He comes into Jerusalem riding on a donkey, and when he sees the city he does not cry out in joy as the crowds around him do, but he weeps saying, "If you, even you, had only recognized on this day the things that make for peace! But now they are hidden from your eyes" (Luke 19:42). They do not understand the political realities before their eyes. And they do not understand the way of God either. For when Jesus enters the temple, he is horrified at the failure of the religious leaders to watch over it as the house of God. He enters the temple and begins to drive out those who are selling things there, and he says, "It is written, 'My house shall be a house of prayer'; but you have made it a den of robbers" (Luke 19:45–6).

As Jesus commences his journey into Jerusalem, the whole multitude of the disciples begins to praise God joyfully with a loud voice for all the deeds of power that they had seen, saying:

> "Blessed is the king
> who comes in the name of the Lord!
> Peace in heaven,
> and glory in the highest heaven!"
>
> *Luke 19:36–7*

This Jesus healed and taught and fed and freed those he encountered who did not hear the voice of God, as he had heard the voice of God, the voice that names us, "Beloved".

But immediately he enters Jerusalem and sees what is happening in the temple of his Father God, he sets up a confrontation with the religious leaders that will lead inexorably to his passion and death.

What sort of a king is this? What sort of saviour?

Today, as we celebrate the feast of Christ the King, our liturgical year comes to a close. Next week is Advent Sunday, and a new liturgical year will begin. This year we have spent time with the Gospel of Luke. During Lent we spent time exploring it looking through the lens of homecoming, one of Luke's key themes. And, tonight, at the end of this year of Luke, we will remember a little of what we found there. The author Brendan Byrne writes of the theme of hospitality in Luke's Gospel:

> "Hospitality" conjures up the context of guests, visitors, putting on meals for them, providing board and lodging, making the stranger feel "at home" in our home ... in this Gospel significant events and exchanges take place in the context of meals and the offering (or non-offering) of hospitality in general. Hospitality... forms a notable frame of reference for the ministry of Jesus. But there is more to it than that. Luke sees the whole life and ministry of Jesus as a *"visitation"* on God's part to Israel and the world. From the start this raises the question: how will this guest, this visitor be *received*? The One who comes as visitor and guest in fact becomes *host* and offers a hospitality in which human beings and, potentially, the entire world, can become truly human, be at home, can *know* salvation in the depth of their hearts.[49]

As we have watched Jesus through the eyes of the writer of Luke's Gospel, we have seen Jesus born through the overshadowing of the Holy Spirit, born of his mother Mary. We have seen Mary assent to bearing God's son—to allowing him a home on this earth. We have seen Jesus who is utterly at home in his Father God, this God who named him "Beloved" at his baptism. All Jesus' earthly life is lived out of his closeness to God. All his encounters with human beings, and his journey to Jerusalem, a journey that ends in death, is walked in God. Jesus lives this life and dies this death that we and all creation too might find our home in God.

Through the year, we have looked at different aspects of Jesus' ministry—his living a life of prayer, infused by the Spirit, prayer through the night on mountains, prayer expressed in rage when his Father's house, the house of prayer is turned into a den of robbers, prayer taught to his disciples in the words of the prayer that bears his name. We have explored his healing, through the faith of those who cry out to him, and through his own compassion. We have witnessed his love of meals with, particularly, those whom society shuns. There are meals with tax collectors and sinners and, most famously in Luke's Gospel, with Zacchaeus, whom Jesus calls down from a tree before inviting himself into Zacchaeus' home. Salvation came to that house that day.

We have wrestled with the parables Jesus told. The Gospel of Luke is where many of Jesus' best-loved parables are found. Following on from the complaints from the religious leaders about the company he keeps, Jesus tells the three parables of the lost—the lost sheep, the lost coin and the Parable of the Prodigal Son. We heard, in the Parable of the Prodigal Son and the Parable of the Dishonest Manager, stories about two characters who, having squandered the life given to them, made extraordinary efforts to get home. And we heard Jesus say through these parables, "Do anything to get home".

It was in the Parable of the Good Samaritan that we heard what is required of us as we journey, and encourage others on that journey, home. When a lawyer asks Jesus to give him some boundary on the concept of neighbour, a neighbour that Jesus told him to love, we found in this parable that the concept of neighbour is a *vocation*. And part of our way home is found in allowing this *vocation to neighbour* to infuse our lives.

Jesus is about salvation. God intends peace for our earth and salvation for all, particularly those on the margins. Mary's song that we hear sung each night at Evensong, leaves us in no doubt that God's embrace is wide and reverses the values of our world. God's project is to bring *all* creation home.

But when Jesus entered Jerusalem, we sensed in the air that God's way of bringing salvation, that the bringing in of God's kingdom, will involve Jesus in terrible suffering. The confrontation with the religious leaders that simmered in the background of so many of the Gospel stories will finally come to the surface. Jesus enters Jerusalem, and there evil will hurl at him its worst.

Jesus walks into the trap that evil sets for him and he looks in the face of every one of the violent men who participate in his trial and who enact his crucifixion, just as he looked the criminals dying beside him in the face too. In his torn body, with his few last breaths, he loves and forgives and looks into the faces of struggling humanity that find itself at his cross.

And then he prays his final prayer. "Father, into your hands I commend my spirit" (Luke 23:46). It is the Spirit that blessed Mary as she assented to be Jesus' mother in Luke's Gospel; it is the Spirit that came upon him at his baptism; it is the Spirit that upheld him throughout his life. And now that Spirit brings him home. His work is done. Creation is redeemed in the love and courage and prayer and in the ruthlessly honest gaze of this dying man. In Christ's Passion redemption is found.

And in Christ's Passion the one we know as king is found.

In the final chapter of Luke's Gospel, we find Jesus and two disciples walking along the Emmaus Road.

On the other side of death, we see Jesus on the Emmaus Road doing all the things he did in his life. We see him keeping company with sinners. We see him hearing the story of their hopes that have been dashed. We see him teaching from the scriptures, and we see him blessing, breaking, sharing bread. We see him alive. We see a Gospel story like all the Gospel stories where death is not the final destination, where Jesus lives and the story of God and God's creation lives on.

And so we'll tell it again shall we? We'll meet next week on Advent Sunday and begin it again. We'll be telling the story through Matthew's eyes, I think we'll find. Each year a different Gospel lens as each year we bring a different lens. We have lived another year after all, a year with joys and struggles, hopes and disappointments, births and deaths, for us and our community, for our country, for the world. We have lived another year of life, of the life God has given us. The key thing is that this life of ours belongs—belongs in the great story of God, in which all our stories find their home.

Dates and Texts of Sermons

Chapter 1: Keeping Watch for Kingfishers
Psalm 139:1–5; Jeremiah 18:1–11
Preached on 4 September 2016.

Chapter 2: Sitting with the Truth
Preached on 1 February 2015.

Chapter 3: Spending Time with God
John 15:1–11
Preached on 6 May 2018.

Chapter 4: Keep Lighting Candles
Acts 1:6–14, John 17:1–11
Preached on 28 May 2017.

Chapter 5: Grace through Goodness—*Middlemarch*
Preached on Lent 1 2014.

Chapter 6: Showing Mercy—
The Grapes of Wrath
Preached on Lent 2 2014.

Chapter 7: Finding Hope—*Bleak House*
Preached on Lent 3 2014.

Chapter 8: Walking in our Shoes—*To Kill a Mockingbird*
Preached on Lent 4 2014.

Chapter 9: They Have No Wine
John 2:1–11
Preached on 17 January 2016.

Chapter 10: Transforming the World
Isaiah 58:1–9a, 1 Corinthians 2:1–12, Matthew 5:13–20
Preached on 5 February 2017.

Chapter 11: Cleansing our Planet
2 Kings 5:1–14; Mark 1:40–5
Preached on 11 February 2018.

Chapter 12: Tell it Slant
Matthew 18:1–14
Preached on 10 September 2017.

Chapter 13: Do Not Be Afraid
Matthew 14:22–33
Preached on 13 August 2017.

Chapter 14: Meeting God in Suffering
Job 42:1–6,10–17; Mark 10:46–52
Preached on 25 October 2015.

Chapter 15: "What Passing-Bells?"—Anzac Centenary
Psalm 23; John 10:11–18
Preached on 26 April 2015.

Chapter 16: Beside a Fire of
Coals—St Peter's Day
Preached on 16 June 2016.

Chapter 17: Pondering Joy
and Pain—Mary
Preached on 14 August 2016.

Chapter 18: Nurturing the
Soul—Music Sunday
Mark 7:24–37
Preached on 20 August 2017.

Chapter 19: Anointing by the Spirit
Preached on Lent 1 2017.

Chapter 20: Healing as Homecoming
Preached on Lent 2 2017.

Chapter 21: Sharing in God's Embrace
Preached on Lent 3 2017.

Chapter 22: Do Anything to Get Home
Preached on Lent 4 2017.

Chapter 23: Heading Home
Preached on Lent 5 2017.

Chapter 24: Whisperings
of Poets and Prophets
Jeremiah 33:14–16; Luke 21:25–36
Preached on 29 November 2015.

Chapter 25: I'll ride with you
Luke 1:26–38
Preached on 21 December 2014.

Chapter 26: Nativity—A
Story Hanging in the Air
Luke 2:41–52
Preached on 27 December 2015.

Chapter 27: Space for our Souls
Preached on 5 March 2017
Matthew 4:1–11

Chapter 28: Behold the
Wood of the Cross
Preached on Good Friday 2018.

Chapter 29: Was it watching
Notre Dame burn?
John 20:1–18
Preached on Easter Day 2019.

Chapter 30: Doubts and
Loves Dig Up the World
John 20:19–31
Preached on 3 April 2016.

Chapter 31: Turning to Christ
Preached on 4 June 2017

Chapter 32: A Loving Community
Preached on 11 June 2017

Chapter 33: Bringing All Creation Home
Preached on 20 November 2016.

Notes

1. Photographer: Ofer Levy.
2. Eugene Peterson, *Under the Unpredictable Plant* (Grand Rapids, MI: William B. Eerdmans Publishing Company, 1992), p. 172.
3. Walter Brueggemann, *Hopeful Imagination* (Philadelphia: Fortress Press, 1986), p. 25.
4. Photograph used by permission of Ofer Levy.
5. "Disclosure" from *Watching for the Kingfisher* by Ann Lewin is © Ann Lewin, 2004, 2006 and 2009. Published by Canterbury Press. Used with permission. rights@hymnsam.co.uk.
6. Walter Brueggemann, *Theology of the Old Testament: An Introduction* (Minneapolis: Fortress Press, 2008), p. 252.
7. Quoted in *Directions*, Newsletter of The Julian Centre, Adelaide, February 2002, editor: the Revd Philip Carter. Used with permission.
8. Words by Clive Sansom, reproduced by permission of David Higham Associates Ltd..
9. Walter Wink, *Engaging the Powers* (Minneapolis: Fortress Press, 1992), p. 6.
10. Charles Dickens, *Bleak House* (London: Penguin Books, 2003), p. x.
11. Michael Fallon, MSC, *The Gospel according to Saint John* (Kensington: Chevalier Press, 1997), p. 81.
12. Fallon, *Gospel according to Saint John*, p. 88.
13. <https://www.theguardian.com/environment/2017/oct/15/david-attenborough-urges-immediate-action-on-plastics-blue-planet>.
14. <http://www.news.com.au/news-story/aed4bfc5d4820312f340255841e8d6a0>.
15. <https://www.youtube.com/watch?v=cX1T79ZKJqM>.
16. Brueggemann, *Hopeful Imagination*), p. 25.
17. THE POEMS OF EMILY DICKINSON: READING EDITION, edited by Ralph W. Franklin, Cambridge, MA: The Belknap Press of Harvard University Press, Copyright © 1998, 1999 by the President and Fellows of Harvard

College. Copyright © 1951, 1955 by the President and Fellows of Harvard College. Copyright © renewed 1979, 1983 by the President and Fellows of Harvard College. Copyright © 1914, 1918, 1919, 1924, 1929, 1930, 1932, 1935, 1937, 1942 by Martha Dickinson Bianchi. Copyright © 1952, 1957, 1958, 1963, 1965 by Mary L. Hampson. Used with permission.

[18] Rowan Williams, *The Edge of Words* (London: Bloomsbury, 2014), p. 149.
[19] Walter Brueggemann *An Introduction to the Old Testament* (Louisville, KY: Westminster John Knox Press, 2003), p. 57.
[20] Rowan Williams, *Meeting God in Mark* (London: SPCK, 2014), pp. 35–6.
[21] John J. Pilch, *Healing in the New Testament: Insights from Medical and Mediterranean Anthropology* (Minneapolis: Fortress Press, 2000).
[22] Brendan Byrne, *The Hospitality of God* (Strathfield: St Pauls Publications, 2000), p. 25.
[23] Byrne, *Hospitality of God*, p. 43.
[24] James Martin, SJ, *The Jesuit Guide to (Almost) Everything: A Spirituality for Real Life* (New York: HarperOne, 2012), p. 8.
[25] Quoted in John Dury, *Painting the Word* (New Haven and London: Yale University Press, 1999), p. 37. Used with permission.
[26] Joachim Jeremias quoted in Robert J. Karris, *Eating Your Way Through Luke's Gospel* (Collegeville, MN: Liturgical Press, 2006), pp. 32–3. Copyright 2006 by Order of Saint Benedict. Published by Liturgical Press, Collegeville, MN. Used with permission.
[27] John Shea, *The Relentless Widow* (Collegeville, MN: Liturgical Press, 2006), pp. 263–271.
[28] Williams, *Edge of Words*, p. 149.
[29] Byrne, *Hospitality of God*, p. 101.
[30] Williams, *Edge of Words*, p. 89.
[31] Williams, *Edge of Words*, p. 90.
[32] #BigRead13: "Why study C. S. Lewis for Lent" with Rowan Williams, *YouTube* video, 7.22. Jan 30, 2013. <https://www.youtube.com/watch?v=K1zBmmyVo0c>.
[33] Brueggemann, *Hopeful Imagination*, pp. 23–4.
[34] Walter Brueggemann, *The Word Militant: Preaching a Decentering Word* (Minneapolis: Fortress Press, 2010), p. 3.
[35] Brueggemann, *The Word Militant*, p. 8.
[36] Brueggemann, *Hopeful Imagination*, p. 41.

37 Michael Mayne, *Dust that Dreams of Glory* (Norwich: Canterbury Press, 2017), pp. 48–9.
38 See Jürgen Moltmann, *The Crucified God* (London: SCM Press, 1974), pp. 251–2.
39 Mayne, *Dust that Dreams of Glory*, p. 60.
40 <https://www.theguardian.com/us-news/2018/mar/14/walkout-students-gun-violence-parkland-florida>.
41 Kitty Ferguson, *Stephen Hawking: Quest for a Theory of Everything* (New York: Bantam Books, 1992), p. 161. Reproduced by permission of The Random House Group Ltd. ©1992.
42 <https://www.theguardian.com/environment/2019/apr/16/greta-thunberg-urges-eu-leaders-wake-up-climate-change-school-strike-movement>.
43 Lucy Winkett, *Our Sound is our Wound* (London: Continuum, 2010), p. 105.
44 James Alison, *Knowing Jesus* (Springfield, IL: Templegate Publishers, 1994), p. 37.
45 Tony Kelly, C.Ss.R, *Behold the Cross* (Liguori, MS: Liguori Publications, 1999), p. 106.
46 Permission to quote given by University of California Press—Books.
47 Alison, *Knowing Jesus*, p. 28.
48 See Alister McGrath, *Theology: The Basics* (Chichester: Wiley-Blackwell, 2012), p. 127.
49 Byrne, *Hospitality of God*, p. 4.

EU GPSR Authorized Representative:

LOGOS EUROPE, 9 rue Nicolas Poussin, 17000 La Rochelle, France

contact@logoseurope.eu

www.ingramcontent.com/pod-product-compliance
Lightning Source LLC
Chambersburg PA
CBHW070554160426
43199CB00014B/2494